LIVING WITHOUT WORRY
J.R. Miller

Living Without Worry

One meets few unworried people. Most faces bear lines of care. Men go anxious to their day's duties, rush through the hours with feverish speed, and bring a hot brain and tumultuous pulse home at night for restless, unrefreshing sleep. This is not only most unsatisfactory, but is also a most costly mode of living.

One night the train lost two hours in running less than a hundred miles. "We have a hot box," was the polite conductor's reply to an impatient passenger who asked to know the cause of the long delays at stations. This hot-box trouble is not altogether unknown in human life. There are many people who move swiftly enough, and with sufficient energy, but who grow feverish, and who are thus impeded in their progress. *A great many failures in life must be charged to worrying.* When a man worries he is impeded in several ways. For one thing, he loses his head. He cannot think clearly. His brain is feverish and will not act at its best. His mind becomes confused, and his decisions are not to be depended upon. The result is, that a worried man never does his work as well as he should do it, or as he could do it if he were free from worry. He is apt to make mistakes.

Worry exhausts vitality. True, all good in life costs. Virtue goes out of us in everything we do that is worth doing. But for normal, healthy action—nature provides. There is recuperative energy enough to supply the waste. The fountain is filled as fast as it is worn away. Worry, however, is abnormal and unhealthy. It exhausts vitality more rapidly than nature can reinforce it. It is like friction in machinery, and grinds away the very fibre of life. Worry, therefore, both impeded progress and makes work unduly costly and exhausting. One neither accomplishes so much, nor does it so well—while the outlay of vitality is greater.

The ideal theory of life is, therefore, work without worry. At least, this certainly ought to be the ideal for a Christian. We have an express command *not to be anxious about anything.* Our whole duty is to do the will of God and leave in his hands the outworking of circumstances, the shaping and overhauling of all the complicated network of influences, so as to bring about the right results. The working plan for a Christian life is clearly laid down in our Lord's words: "Seek first the kingdom of God, and his righteousness; and all these things shall be added unto you." "Don't worry about tomorrow, for tomorrow will bring its own worries. Today's trouble is enough for today." This ideal leaves no place whatever for worry. It requires single-hearted devotion to the interests of Christ's kingdom, the elimination of self and self-seeking, uncompromising loyalty to the principles of righteousness, and the faithful and energetic doing of duty—all duty, without regard to pleasure or cost. This is all the human part. Then God will look after the outcome; will take care of us and of the results of our acts. It is the function of faith, when we have done what we can, to put all into the divine hands, giving ourselves no anxiety, while we go forward in peace and confidence to the next duty that awaits.

It is said of a Christian man, who has risen from a humble station to great national prominence, that his motto has always been: "Do the very best you can, and leave the rest to Providence." This is nothing more or less than the putting into plain, crisp Saxon, our Lord's counsel already quoted. If we would all get this bit of practical heavenly wisdom out of our New Testament and into our daily life, it would not only greatly increase our working capacity, and consequently make us more successful, but it would also largely enhance our happiness.

We must notice, however, that this is not a labor-saving ideal for life. It is not a theory for an indolent man. It implies the putting of all life's skill and energy into every piece of work we perform; we are to do always the very best we can. We should train ourselves to bring all our wisdom and all our power even to the smallest tasks. We should learn to decide promptly, and always according to the best light we can get at the moment from all our experience and all our knowledge of the subject, and then to act swiftly, energetically, and with all the skill we can command. When we have so acted, the matter is out of our hands, and should be left to the divine out-working, without a misgiving or an anxious thought. We have done our best in the circumstances, and we know that is all we are ever required to do.

But may we not sometimes decide unwisely? Even with our best and ripest wisdom, may we not make mistakes of judgment? Certainly we may. But even when it appears afterward that our decision was not the wisest that might have been made, we should still refuse to worry over it. We did the best we knew, and that is as far as our responsibility goes. We could have done no better in the circumstances, with our light. *We have a right to believe that he who orders all events, will use even our mistake, overruling it in some way for good, if we but leave it in his hands.*

Then why should be worry about that which we cannot change, since it has passed beyond our control? We ought to regret our sins and the mistakes which come from our own follies, though even in such cases we should not waste time in tears which ought to be given to amendment. But when we have done our best, with prayer and holy purpose, we have no right to fret and vex ourselves. Perhaps what seems to us to have been unwise was, after all, God's truer wisdom setting ours aside.

So there is really no place in a true, earnest, Christian life for worry. *Do your very best in the circumstances, and leave the rest with God.* We should aim only to be faithful in duty, and then be at peace, whatever may come. We should work without worrying.

But this is one of those great life lessons which must be *learned.* It never comes naturally. The capacity for learning it, and the needful help is given, but we must learn the lesson ourselves, just as we learn other lessons. The process must always be slow; no one can in a single day learn to live and work without worry. Usually is requires years. Yet much can be accomplished by everyone who is willing to endure the necessary discipline. We must first accept the truths of the gospel on which the lesson rests, and must believe them—that *duty alone is ours, and that results and out-workings are God's.* Then we must begin firmly and heroically to practice the lesson, to live by it, to train ourselves to confident, peaceful living.

The lesson is well worth learning, at whatever cost. To live nobly, energetically, up to one's best, and yet without worry, is one of the highest attainments possible. It is the ideal life. It is the life whose vision of beauty is pictured for us in the peace which our Lord promises his people, the peace that passes all understanding that keeps the heart and mind in Christ Jesus—the perfect peace that comes to him whose mind is stayed on God.

Starting Right

"The *beginning* is half of the whole," says an old proverb. A good *start* is a move in the direction of success. No time need then be wasted in *revising* plans, in *correcting* mistakes, or in changing one's course. No steps need then be retraced. There are no wrong teachings to unlearn; no false systems to abandon. One's whole energy can be given to the carrying out of one's chosen purpose.

On the other hand, many a career of brilliant possibilities is marred by *a wrong beginning*. There are mistakes of early days which men never get over. The latter half of many a life—is spent in undoing, or vainly trying to undo, the acts of its former half. A bad foundation has caused the wreck of many a noble building. Inadequate preparation for a business or a calling, leads to impaired success at the best, and most frequently it results in utter failure.

The same principles apply in Christian life. It is of the utmost importance that we start well. Many Christian walk in doubt and shadow all their days, never entering into joy and peace, because at the beginning they fail to understand the fullness of the blessedness into which, as children of God, they come when they receive Christ. Many others never attain anything noble and beautiful in Christian life and character, because they do not, at the beginning, wholly disentangle themselves from their old life, and make a full dedication of themselves to Christ. A good beginning, therefore, involves two things:
first, clearness and definiteness of aim, with intelligent views of what it is to be a Christian;
second, completeness of consecration.

Many men fail in life—because they have no **settled purpose**, no **well-defined plan**. They have no goal set before them which they strive to reach. There is no ideal in their mind toward which they mean to struggle. They merely *drift* on the current, and are borne by it wherever it flows. They are not *masters* in life, but poor *slaves*. They conquer nothing, but are the mere passive creatures of circumstances. Such a life is unworthy of an intelligent being with immortal powers; nor does it ever reach any high degree of nobleness or success.
No *sculptor* ever touches the marble until he has in his mind a definite conception

of his work as it will be when finished. He sees a vision before him, of a very lovely form—and then sets to work to fashion the vision in stone. No builder begins to erect a house until a complete plan, embracing every detail, has been adopted and prepared. He knows precisely what the finished structure will be before he strikes a stroke. No one would cut into a web of rich and costly cloth—until he had before him the pattern of the garment he would like to make. In all work on material things, men have definite aims, and they know precisely what they intend to produce before they begin their work. But in life itself and living—all do not exercise such wisdom. Many never give a thought to such questions as these: "What is the purpose of my life? What ought I to do with it? What should be the great aim of my existence? What should I strive to be, and to do?"

Multitudes live aimlessly, having no thought of the responsibility of living, and never forming any earnest, resolute purpose to rise to any noble height, or to achieve any worthy or beautiful thing. But a true life should always have its *aim*. To grow up as a *plant*—without thinking—is well enough for a plant; but *men* with immortal souls and measureless possibilities should have a purpose, and should seek to attain it. No one begins well or worthily in life—who has not settled in his own mind what he will strive to do with his life.

In entering upon a Christian life, there should always be a clear aim. We should know definitely what it is to be a Christian. With only vague ideas of the meaning of a Christian life, its aim, its requirements, its privileges, its duties—no one can begin well. We need to understand the new relations into which we come as children of God, so that we may realize the full blessedness of our position in Christ. We need to have a clear conception of the final aim of all Christian attainment, so that we may strive toward it. We need to know what is required of a Christian, toward his God and toward his fellow-men, that we may faithfully and intelligently take up every duty. We need to know the conditions of Christian life, in order that we may avail ourselves of the necessary helps provided for us. Thus a clear and intelligent aim, is essential in starting right as a Christian.

Another essential element—is the **devotion and consecration of ourselves to the life we have chosen**. A good aim is not enough. One may aim an arrow with perfect accuracy, but the bow must also be drawn and the cord let fly—if the arrow is to reach the mark. A vision in the brain is not enough for the sculptor; he must hew the vision into form in the marble. The architect's plan is only a picture, and there must be toil and cost—until the building stands complete in its noble beauty. A good *aim* is not all of a Christian life. It is nothing more than an *empty dream*— unless it is wrought out in the life. When Raphael was asked how he painted his marvelous pictures, he replied, "I dream dreams and I see visions—and then I paint my dreams and my visions." Every earnest Christian who looks much at Christ, dreams dreams and sees visions—dreams and visions of wondrous beauty, glimpses of the loveliness of Christ; and, like the artist, he should seek with patient, yet intense purpose—to reproduce the loveliness in his own soul. Many people have sublimest *aspirations* and *intentions*—who never take a step toward the *realization* of them. *Mere knowing* what it is to be a Christian, makes no one a

Christian; many perish with the glorious ideal shining fully and clear before their eyes. Mere seeing the beauty of Christ as it is held before us for our copying—will never fashion us into that beauty. Our knowledge must be wrought into life. We must carve out in our life—the beauty we see.

We all need to start anew very often. The best purposes need frequent reforming. The intensest energy needs often rekindling. What better new beginning can there be than a fresh look at a life's true aim, and a fresh consecration to the working out of that aim?

Thinking and Turning

It was one of the old Psalm writers who said, "I *thought* on my ways." It is not likely that he found it a very easy thing to do. It is usually very much harder to think on our own ways—than on other people. Most of us do quite enough of the latter. We keep a *magnifying glass* to inspect our neighbor's life, a high-power microscope to hunt for specks in his character; but too often we forget to use our glasses on ourselves, or, if we do, we reverse them, and thus minimize our every spot and imperfection. The Pharisee in the temple confessed a great many sins, but they were his neighbor's sins and the publican's sins; he made no confession at all for himself. Most of us are in the same danger. We like to think of our ways when they are good—it flatters our vanity to be able to approve and commend ourselves; but when our conduct has not been particularly satisfactory, we like to turn our backs upon it, and solace ourselves by thinking on our neighbor's naughty ways. And here, strange to say, it seems to please many of us best—to find things we cannot approve or commend in others.

It is a brave thing for a man to say, "I will think upon *my own* ways," and says it when he knows his ways have not been good and right, but wrong. It is an excellent thing for us to turn our lenses in upon our own hearts, in order to see if our own ways are right. There is only one person in all the world for whose ways any of us are really responsible, for whose life any of us must give account—and that is one's self. Other people's wrong ways may pain us and offend ours sense of right; and it is our duty to do all we can, in the spirit of Christ, to lead our neighbors into better ways. But, after all, when we stand before God's judgment-seat, the only one person in the whole world for which any one of us will have to give account—will be one's self. Certainly it is most important, then, that we give earnest heed to ourselves, and our own ways.

A *review* of one's life, has a strange power. As we look back upon our ways, they do not appear to us as they did when we were passing through them. Things which seemed hard and painful at the time, now, as we look back upon them, appear lovely and radiant. There are experiences in most lives, which seemed to be *calamities* at the time—but in the end prove rich *blessings*. Then there is another class—things which appear attractive and enjoyable at the time, which afterward look repulsive and abhorrent. This is true of all wrong actions, all deeds wrought under the influence of wrong passion. At the time they give a thrill of pleasure; but when the emotions had passed, and the wrong-doer turns and looks back at what he has done—it seems horrible in his eyes. The retrospect fills him with disgust and loathing.

To look at one's ways when they have been wrong, is not by any means a pleasant thing to do. Such looks, if honest, will produce deep sorrow. It is well that it should be so—that regret should grow into sore pain, until it has burned into our hearts the lessons which we ought to learn from our *follies* and *sins*. But pain and regret should not be all. The Scriptures speak of the sorrow of the world—which works death. This is a sorrow which passes away like the morning cloud or the early dew, leaving no impression, or the sorrow which ends only in despair. *Godly sorrow* is the pain for sins which leads to repentance.

The *prodigal* in the far-off land thought on his ways, and, in his shame, hid his face in his hands, and wept bitter tears over the ruin he had made of his life. But he did more than weep; he rose, and went straight home to his father. No matter how badly one has failed, the noblest thing to do is, not to sit down and waste other years in grieving over the lost years. Weeping in the darkness of despair, amends nothing. The only truly wise thing is to rise, and save what remains. Because ten hours out of the twelve allotted are lost, shall we sit down and waste the other two in unavailing grief over the ten? Had we not better to use the two which are left, in doing what we can to retrieve the consequences of our past folly?

"We have lost the battle," said Napoleon, "but," drawing his watch from his pocket, "it is only two o'clock, and we have time to fight and win another"; and the sun went down on a victorious army. No young person, especially, should ever yield to despair; for in youth there is yet too wide a margin to blot with the confession of defeat and failure. Even old age, with a whole lifetime behind it wasted, is not hopeless in a world on which Christ's cross stood. A few moments are enough in which to creep to Christ's feet and find pardon. Life does not end at the grave. Its path sweeps on into the eternal years, and there will be time enough then to retrieve all the wasted past. Someone speaks of heaven, as the place where God makes over souls. Even lives only wasted and marred on earth, turning to Christ in the late evening-time of life, may find mercy, and in heaven's long blessed day be made over into grace and beauty.

But nothing comes of thinking on our ways—if we do not *turn* from whatever we find to be wrong. Godly sorrow works *repentance*. A few tears amount to nothing, if one goes on tomorrow in the same old paths. Someone says: "The true science of blundering consists in never making the same mistake twice." This rule applies to sins as well as to mistakes. The true science of living, is never to commit the same sin a second time. But even this falls short. We are not saved by negatives. We can never go to heaven by merely turning from wrong ways. True repentance leads to Christ, and into his ways. It is the man who forsakes his wicked ways and wicked thoughts, and returns to the Lord—who is abundantly pardoned. It does not matter how black the sins are—when there is this kind of repentance. Even Christ does not undo the wrong past, and make that which has been done—as though it never had been done. But grace may so make over a marred life, that, where the blemish was—some special beauty may appear. "The oyster mends its shell with a pearl." Where the ugly wound was—there comes, with the healing, not a scar—but a pearl.

The same is true in human souls, when divine grace heals the wounds of sin. Sins that we truly repent of, become pearls in the character. It is the experience of all whose lives grow into Christ-like nobleness, that many of the golden lines of their later lives have been wrought out by their regrets and their repenting of wrongdoings. Even our mistakes and sins, if we leaven them and find our way to Christ, will be transmuted into growth and up building of character. "We can so deal with the past—that we can make it give up to us virtue and wisdom." "We can make wrong—the seed of right and righteousness; we can transmute error into wisdom; we can make sorrow bloom into a thousand forms, like fragrant flowers." That is, if we truly repent of our sins, where they grew with their thorns and poison seeds, there will be in our lives—trees and plants of beauty with sweet flowers and rich fruits.

Sins of Omission

There are *sins of not doing*. We are not accustomed to look at our *sins of omission* as we do at our sins of *commission*. We call it a sin when one does another an injury—but we are not so likely to call it a sin when one fails to show another, when in suffering or in need, a kindness which it was in his power to render. Yet, in God's sight, it is a grievous sin to *withhold* the good which it is in our power to do.

This is taught in a most striking way by our Lord in his representation of the last judgment. To those on his *left* hand the King will say, "Depart from me, you who are cursed, into the eternal fire prepared for the devil and his angels. For I was hungry and you gave me nothing to eat, I was thirsty and you gave me nothing to drink, I was a stranger and you did not invite me in, I needed clothes and you did not clothe me, I was sick and in prison and you did not look after me." Matthew 25:41-43. There are no sins of *commission* charged against these condemned people. It is not said that they were liars, or dishonest; that they were unjust, cruel, or inhuman; that they oppressed the poor, crushed the weak, defrauded the orphan and the widow. All that is said of them is that they did *not* feed the hungry, did *not* give drink to the thirsty, did *not* provide hospitable shelter to the stranger, did *not* clothe the naked, and did *not* visit the sick or the prisoner. They were condemned for *not doing* the things of love, that awaited for them day by day. Terrible is the arraignment, too, and terrible the judgment: "Depart from me, you cursed ones, into the eternal fire which is prepared for the devil and his angels," — because you have *not done* the things of love that made their appeal to you.

We are slow to accept this teaching. At the close of a day we examine ourselves, and review the day's record, to find wherein we have done wrong. We remember the hasty word we spoke, which gave pain to a tender heart, and confess it. We recall with penitence our self-indulgence, our lapses from truth, honesty, or integrity, even our breaches of courtesy. But, in counting up the sins of the day, do we think with regret or pain of *the things we did not do?* Are we penitent for our sins of omission? We have "passed by on the other side" of many a human need and hunger. Do we confess these sins at the ending of the day?

A young man came to Jesus to ask him the way of life. He was a good man. His life had been blameless and stainless from his youth. He was honored and respected among men. His character was so beautiful that Jesus, beholding him, loved him. Yet he told him frankly that there was a lack. And the fault was not in the things he had *done*—but in the things he had *not done*—a "lack," something wanting. The young man was bidden, if he would be perfect, if he would make his life complete—to sell all he had and give to the poor. No doubt there are many people everywhere who live well, whose character is unblemished, whose life is blameless, against whom no one can bring any accusation—but in whom there is a great lack, almost a whole hemisphere of their life blank and empty!

The lesson is needed in our homes. We live together as families perhaps quite lovingly. The fathers are good providers, the mothers are good housekeepers, the parents care well for their children's education and other interests, the children live together in reasonable harmony and good fellowship. Yet there is a lack in the household life. The things that are done may be beyond criticism, almost ideal—but there is something lacking in the family fellowship, in things that are *not* done which ought to be done.

Sometimes love's duties are crowded out by other seeming duties. There are men so absorbed in their business and in their outer-world life that they have little strength or time left for the cultivation of the home life, and for their duties of love to those who are dearest. In all their relations they are kindly and generous—but there is a lack. They do not minister to the heart-needs of their household.

There are *mothers* who are so busied with social duties and other outside engagements, that they leave undone many things which would have blessed the world far more than the things they do. These outside things may be important in their way. Christian women have a mission to society. Yet their first and holiest duty is ever to their own home. Whatever work may call a woman outside, whatever needs of other homes may appeal to her; she cannot be excused from the duties she owes to the loved ones of her own household. These are her own duties, and no other one's. If she does not do them, they must go undone. No other woman can be mother to her children. Outside needs appeal to others as well as to her—but the things of her home are hers alone. It will be very sad, therefore, if she omits the duties of love within her own doors, while she is doing things outside, however important they may be.

It is the sins of *omission* which are likely to do the greatest harm in family life—the gentle words which lie on our tongues—but which we do not speak; the kindly acts which we feel the impulse to perform—but which we do not perform; the thoughtful things which we might have done, to give cheer and comfort—but which we did not do. We say that *silence is golden*, and sometimes it is. It is golden when the word that was near being spoken, would have been a hasty word—sharp, cutting, bitter. But silence is not golden when the word which is in our heart is loving, cheering, comforting, and inspiring. We surely wrong our loved ones when we withhold such a word.

We are told that we must give an account for every *idle* word we speak—but someone reminds us that we must give account as well for our *idle silences*. Reserve is a good thing in its place; but when it is love which is kept in reserve, and in one's own home, reserve becomes cruelty, robbery. We need to make sure, as we pass along, that no one of our household can ever say to us, "I was hungry-hearted, and you gave me no daily bread of love. I was thirsty for human sympathy, and you gave me no drink. I was a stranger at your heart's door, and you took me not into love's warmth and shelter. I was sick with life's burdens and sorrows, and you ministered not to me from your rich store. I was in prison in my narrow environment, and you did not come to me with companionship that I craved. Living by my side all these years, you did not do love's duty to me." Among the most grievous sins against those who are nearest and dearest to us—are the sins of omission.

But not in the home alone is the lesson needed; there is the same danger in all life's relations. "You shall love your *neighbor* as yourself." Because a man does not defraud nor inflict bodily hurt upon his neighbor; has he therefore met all the requirements of the divine law? To love a man is a great deal more than not wronging or injuring him.

All along life's dusty wayside, lie men and women who are wounded, hurt, robbed, and left to die. We are continually going by them. Do we pass by on "the other side"? You learned the other morning of a *neighbor* in trouble. It was your thought to go to him with help. But you did not do it. He bows, in the evening, in the deep darkness, beneath his burden, crushed, almost in despair. He might have been rejoicing, had it not been for your sin of omission. There was a *young man* in sore temptation. The battle was for his very soul. You knew of it, and meant to find him, and say a brave word to him. But you were busy, and did not go. The young man fell—fell because you did not take him a brother's help.

It is not enough that we commit no evil against others—we must watch lest we fail to do them the good which is in our power to do. We shall be judged, not alone by what we *do*—but quite as much by what we leave *undone*. We need to give heed, not alone to our sins of *commission*—but also to our sins of *omission*.

The Lesson of Joy

Joy is God's ideal for his children. The Christian is exhorted to *rejoice always*. This does not mean that his life is exempt from trouble. The gospel does not give us a new set of conditions, with pain and sorrow eliminated. Christian joy is something that overcomes sorrow.

There are many things which are meant to minister joy. This is a *beautiful world* in which we live. We do not think enough about what God has done for our pleasure in the adorning of our earthly home. Many have said that, when Jesus speaks of the many mansions in the Father's house, he does not refer to heaven only—but means that this world is one of the mansions, while heaven is another. Surely it is beautiful enough for an apartment of the Father's house. No doubt heaven will be more lovely, for sin has left its trail on everything of earth. Yet there is loveliness enough in this world to fill our hearts with rapture.

Another thing which ministers to human joy is the *goodness of God in providence.* The world is not only beautiful; it is our Father's world. Jesus says that our Father feeds even the birds, and clothes even the flowers; and he assures us that his care for his children is much more tender and sure. "If I could not believe," says one, "that there is a thinking mind at the center of things, life would be to me intolerable." But there is not only a thinking mind—there is also a *Father's heart* at the center of things. On every leaf is written a covenant of divine love. On every flower and tuft of moss, is found a pledge of divine thought and faithfulness.

It would minister greatly to our joy, if we had a firmer faith in the *goodness of the providence which rules in life's affairs.* It is said that one of the great diamond fields of South Africa was discovered in this interesting way: One day a traveler entered the valley and paused before a settler's door where a boy was amusing himself by throwing little stones. One of the stones fell at the feet of the visitor, and he picked it up and was about to return it to the boy when he saw a flash of light from it which arrested his attention and made his heart beat with eager surprise. The stone was a diamond. The boy had no thought of its value. To him it was only a plaything. To the passer-by it was only a common pebble, which he spurned with his foot. But to the eye of the man of science, it was a gem of surpassing value was enfolded in the rough covering. All the pebbles scattered about were also diamonds.

Many of the events of Providence appear to ordinary eyes, as uninteresting, unmeaning, and often even unkindly. Yet in each, there is wrapped up a divine treasure of good and blessing for the child of God. We need only *eyes of faith* to find in every painful experience, a helper of our joy. Precious gems of rarest blessing, are enclosed in the rough crusts of hardship, care, loss, and trial—which we are continually coming upon in life's ways.

Another helper of joy is a *happy home*. Many of us would never be able, day after day, to face life with its struggles, its duties, its antagonisms, were it not for the renewal of strength which we get in our home. A true home is a little fragment of heaven let down on earth, to inspire us with patience and strength for the way.

A *godly life* also ministers to joy. One who neglects and disobeys God's commandments, is making unhappiness for himself. Sin's pleasures yield briers and thorns. The later years of life are fields in which the sowings of earlier years come to ripeness. Nothing ministers more surely to happiness, than a well-watched past. Good deeds, gentle ministries, unselfish kindnesses, yield memories of joy.

There is a Persian story of a vizier who dedicated one apartment in his palace to be a chamber of memory. In this he kept the memorials of his earlier days, before royal favor had lifted him from his lowly place to honor. It was a little room with bare floor, and here he kept his crook, his wallet, his coarse dress, and his water-cruse—the things which had belonged to his shepherd life. Every day he went for an hour from the splendors of his palace to this humble apartment, to live again for a time amidst the memories of his happy youth. Very sweet were his recollections, and by this daily visit, his heart was kept warm and tender amid all the pomp and show, and all the trial and sorrow of his public life.

It would be a wonderful promoter of joy if everyone, in the midst of life's responsibilities and cares, its temptations and struggles, would keep such a chamber of memory filled with the mementoes of his youth's happy days. Most of us grow old too soon. We forget our childhood joys, and we take upon us too early the burdens of maturity. We should keep one room in our heart as a treasure-chamber for the sweet joys that we have left behind. Memory has a marvelous power to make joy for us.

These are some of the ways in which joy is promoted. The word "glad" comes from a root which means to be bright, to shine. Much is said in the Bible about the duty of Christians to be lights in the world. We are lamps which God lights, that we may shine. We are particularly warned against having our light dimmed or obscured. Nothing does this more effectually than unhappiness. A Christian should be a lamp which always shines. A man who had lived an unusually long and noble Christian life, feared that he might fail to honor Christ in suffering. Many Christians fail at this point. When trials come, the brightness grows dim. We forget that it is as sinful to lose our joy and peace—as it is to lose our honesty and truthfulness.

Joy is not a mere privilege for a Christian, a quality which he may or may not have in his life. It is not a matter merely of temperament. It will not do to say that, while some people were born with a sunny spirit, we were born with a gloomy disposition, and therefore cannot be joyful. It is the mission of Christian faith, to change nature. "The fruit of the Spirit is *joy*." Christian joy is not natural exhilaration—it is converted sadness.

How can we learn to be always glad-hearted? *Atmosphere* is important. If we live in a malarial region, we need not be surprised if we have malaria. If we move to a place where there is pure, sweet, wholesome air—we may hope to be well and strong. There are spiritual atmospheres, too, some wholesome, some unwholesome, and we should choose our abiding-place where the influences will promote joy. Too many Christians live in the fog and fear of unbelief, and then wonder why they do not have the joy of the Lord.

Far more than we know, is joy a lesson to be learned. It does not come naturally to many of us, at least, although there is a great difference in temperament, and some learn the lesson much more easily than others do. To none is it natural to rejoice in sorrow—this is something which all of us must learn. Nor can we merely, by resolving to be glad, go through all the days thereafter with a song in our heart and sunshine in our face. The lesson can be mastered only through years of patient self-discipline, just as all life's lessons must be mastered.

It will help us in this experience, if we keep ever before us the ideal that we are always to be joyful, that failure here is sin, and grieves God. It will help us, also, if we keep our heart full of the great thoughts which are meant to inspire joy. Longfellow gave a young friend this advice: "See some good picture—in nature, if possible, or on canvas—hear a page of the best music, or read a great poem every day. Then, at the end of the year, your mind will shine with such an accumulation of jewels, as will astonish even yourself." To this may be added: Take into your heart every day some cheering Word of God. Listen to some heavenly song of hope or joy. Let your eye dwell on some beautiful vision of divine love. Thus your very soul will become a fountain of light, and joy will become more and more the dominant mood of your life.

We cannot too strongly emphasize the truth, that joy is a Christian duty. We are here to lighten the world by our life. This we can never do, by going about with sad face and heavy heart. If our religion cannot make us rejoicing Christians, whatever our temperament, or whatever our circumstances may be, we are not getting the best from it. We cannot serve the world so well in any other way—as by being joyful Christians. Then the light will shine through us wherever we go, and others who witness the victoriousness of our life will want to know of the Savior, who can help us to such triumphant faith.

Can We Learn to Be Contented?

Someone has said that if men were to be saved by contentment, instead of by faith in Christ, most people would be lost. Yet contentment is possible. There was one man at least who said, and said it very honestly, "I have *learned* in whatever state I am, therein to be content." His words have special value, too, when we remember in what circumstances they were written. They were dated in a prison, when the writer was wearing a chain. It is easy enough to say such things in the *summer days of prosperity*—but to say them amid trials and adversities, requires a real experience of victorious living.

But just what did Paul mean when he said, "I am content"? The original word, scholars tell us, contains a fine sense which does not come out into the English translation. It means *self-sufficing*. Paul, as a Christian man, had in himself all that he needed to give him tranquility and peace. Therefore he was not dependent upon any external circumstances. Wherever he went, there was in himself a competence, a fountain of supply, a self-sufficing. This is the true secret of Christian contentment wherever it is found. We cannot keep sickness, pain, sorrow, and misfortune away from our lives—yet as Christians we are meant to live in any experience in unbroken peace, in sweet restfulness of soul.

How may this unbroken contentment be obtained? Paul's description of his own life, gives us a hint as to the way he reached it. He says, "I have *learned* to be content." It is no small comfort to us common people, to get this from such a man. It tells us that even with him, it was not always thus; that at first he probably chafed amid discomforts, and had to "learn" to be contented in trial. It did not come naturally to him, any more than it does to the rest of us, to have peace in the heart, in time of external strife. Nor did this beautiful way of living come to him at once as a divine gift when he became a Christian. He was not miraculously helped to acquire contentment. It was not a special power granted to him as an apostle.

He tells us plainly in his old age, that he has "learned" it. This means that he was not always able to say, "I am content in any state." This was an attainment of his later years, and he reached it by struggle and by discipline, by learning in the school of Christ, just as all of us have to learn it if we ever do, and as any of us may learn it if we will.

Surely everyone who desires to grow into spiritual beauty, should seek to learn this lesson. Discontent is a miserable fault. It grieves God, for it springs from a lack of faith in him. It destroys one's own heart-peace; discontented people are always unhappy. It disfigures beauty of character. It sours the temper, ruffles the calm of sweet life, and tarnishes the loveliness of the spirit. It even works out through the flesh, and spoils the beauty of the fairest face. To have a transfigured face, one must have heaven in one's heart. Just in proportion as the lesson is learned, are the features brightened by the outshining of the indwelling peace. Besides all this, discontent casts shadows on the lives of others. One discontented person in a family, often makes a whole household wretched. If not for our own sake, then, we ought at least for the sake of our friends to learn to be contented. We have no right to cast shadows on other lives.

But how can we learn contentment? One step toward it is patient submission to unavoidable ills and hardships. No earthly lot is perfect. No mortal in this world, ever yet found a set of circumstances without some drawback. Sometimes it lies in our power to remove the discomfort. Much of our hardship is of our own making. Much of it would require but a little energy on our own part to cure. We surely are very foolish if we live on amid ills and frets, day after day, which we might change for comforts if we would. All removable troubles we ought, therefore, to remove. But there are trials which we cannot change into pleasures, burdens which we cannot lay off, crosses which we must continue to carry, and "thorns in the flesh" which must remain with their rankling. When we have such trials, why should we not sweetly accept them as part of God's best way with us? Discontent never made a rough path smoother, a heavy burden lighter, a bitter cup less bitter, a dark way brighter, a sorrow less sore. It only makes matters worse. One who accepts with patience what he cannot change, has learned the secret of victorious living.

Another part of the lesson is that we moderate our desires. Paul says, "If we have food and clothing—we will be content with these." 1 Timothy 6:8. Very much of our discontent arises from envy of those who seem to be more favored than ourselves. Many people lose most of the comfort out of their own lot, in coveting the finer things some neighbor has. Yet if they knew the whole story of the life they envy for its greater prosperity, they probably would not exchange for it their own lowlier life, with its homelier circumstances. Or if they could make the exchange, it is not likely they would find half so much real happiness in the other position, as they had enjoyed in their own. Contentment does not dwell so often in palaces—as in the homes of the humble. The tall peaks rise higher and are more conspicuous—but the winds smite them more fiercely than they do the quiet vales. And surely the lot in life which God makes for us—is always the very best that could be made for us for the time being. The cause of our discontent is not in our circumstances; if it were, a change might cure it. It is in ourselves; and, wherever we go, we shall carry it with us.

Envious desires for other people's places which seem finer than ours, prevent our getting the best blessing and good out of our own. Trying to grasp the things which are beyond our reach, we leave unseen, unappreciated, untouched, and despised, the many sweet bits of happiness which lie close about us. Someone says: "Stretching out his hand to catch the stars, man forgets the flowers at his feet, so beautiful, so fragrant, so multitudinous, and so various." A fine secret of contentment lies in finding and extracting all the pleasure we can get from the things we have, while we enter no mad, vain chase after impossible dreams. In whatever state we are, we may therein find enough for our need.

If we would learn the lesson of contentment, we must train ourselves to live for the higher things. One of the ancient wise men, having heard that a storm had destroyed his merchant ships, thus sweeping away all his fortune, said: "It is just as well, for now I can give up my mind more fully to study." He had other and higher sources of enjoyment, than his merchandise, and felt the loss of his ships no more than manhood feels the loss of childhood's toys. He was but a heathen philosopher; we are Christians. He had only his studies to occupy his thought when his property was gone; and we have all the blessed things of God's love. No earthly misfortune can touch the wealth a Christian holds in the divine promises and hopes.

Just in the measure, therefore, in which we learn to live for spiritual and eternal realities—do we find contentment amid earth's trials and losses. If we live to please God, to build up Christlike character in ourselves, and to lay up treasure in heaven—we shall not depend for happiness on the way things go with us here on earth, nor on the measure of temporal goods we have. The lower desires are crowded out by the higher. We can do without *childhood's toys* when we have manhood's better possessions; we need this world less as we get more of God and heaven into our hearts.

This was the secret of the contentment of the old prisoner whose immortal word is so well worth considering. He was content in any trial, because earth meant so little and Christ meant so much to him. He did not need the things he did not have; he was not made poor by the things he had lost; he was not vexed by the sufferings he had to endure, because the sources of his life were in heaven, and could not be touched by earthly experiences of pain or loss.

These are hints of the way we may learn in whatever state we are therein to be content. Surely the lesson is worth learning. One year of sweet content, amid earth's troublous scenes, is better than a lifetime of vexed, restless discontent. The lesson can be learned, too, by anyone who truly is Christ's disciple, for did not the Master say: "Peace I leave with you; my peace I give unto you"?

The artist painted life as a dark, storm-swept sea filled with wrecks. Then out on the wild sea-waves, he made a rock to arise, in a cleft of which, high up, amid herbage and flowers, he painted a dove sitting quietly on her nest. It is a picture of Christian peace in the midst of this world's strifes and storms. In the cleft of the rock is the home of content.

Building Our Life on God's Plan

God has a plan for every life. This plan is in God's mind before the person is born. The divine Creator never brings a human soul into being and starts it on its immortal destiny, without knowing precisely what place he means it to fill in this world, what work he means it to do, what he means it to become. The plan is not the same for any two lives; there is a special purpose for each one. We reach our highest success in life and do the noblest work possible for us to do—when we discover what God's thought is for us, and try our best to work it out.

It certainly must be possible, too, for us to learn what God's plan is for our own life. God would never be so unreasonable as to require and expect certain things of us— and not be willing and ready to tell us what they are. He would not have a pattern for us to follow—and then hide it out of sight so that we cannot see it. He will show us the pattern if we look for it at the right place, and if we are really ready to accept it and make it our own.

It will be a pity if any of us disregard God's thought and purpose for our life, and ignore it, and make one of our own instead—a poor, imperfect, short-sighted, faulty plan—instead of God's noble, wise, perfect, and beautiful plan. It would be as if the mere builder of the cathedral should throw aside the great wise architect's plan—

and take his own poor ignorant idea instead. It would be a pity if we have a divine plan for our life lying close beside us, within our reach, so that we can see it and follow it—if we should yet fail to see it, and, wondering what God wants us to do, what his purpose is for us, and wishing we might know—and should go stumbling on in darkness, only guessing at the way and at our duty.

God shows us our life's pattern, in his Word. He leads us to these Holy Scriptures and there lets us see patterns for every part of the *building of character* which he wants us to rear. So there is urgent necessity for a constant *reading* and *pondering* and deep *study* of the Bible—if we would discover the plans and patterns for our life which God has prepared. Imagine the builders working away on a cathedral day by day, without referring to the architect's drawings—just building haphazard, as the fancy struck them. What a struggling, shapeless, mongrel pile, the house would be in the end! Like this would be the life-fabric which one would pile up who did not study the Bible, to find there the *Lord's patterns for his life.*

Again, God shows us his plans for our life—in other holy lives. Every glimpse of spiritual loveliness we see in a Christian friend or in any saintly character, is a pattern shown to us which we are to seek to work into our own life. When we see sweet patience in a sufferer, peace in one who is in sore trial, quiet meekness in one who is enduring injuries, cheerfulness in one who is passing through afflictions—God is letting us see gleams and glimpses of what he wants us to be, and the way he wants us to live. Especially as we take our New Testament and study the life and the character of Christ, do we see the perfect pattern. In the best human lives we have only single *gleams* of spiritual loveliness—perhaps gentleness; or courage; or sympathy—mingled with faults and imperfections almost hiding the beauty—a little flower amid a cluster of briers or thorns, a lily growing out of a black bog. But in Christ we see all the qualities of a perfect life, in their richest, ripest loveliness, without a fault or a flaw. As we behold Christ, therefore, we are looking upon the one perfect pattern.

There are questions of duty, which are not directly answered in the Bible. So far as a matter of character, disposition, temper, spirit, and conduct are concerned—we need no other guide than Scripture. The plans for our life are all there. But the Bible does not tell a young man what business or calling to choose. It does not tell him where he should locate to conduct his business or pursue his profession. It does not tell a young woman what education will benefit her for her life-work. It does not show us which of two courses to choose when we stand at a dividing of the ways. It does not tell men what investments to make, when to buy or sell property. It does not show us just what to do when we are brought face to face with responsibilities, and cannot be sure of the best thing. Sometimes we hear of people opening the Bible and taking the first verse that their eye falls on as an answer to their question, or as a guiding hand in their perplexity. That is only *superstition*. The Bible is not meant to be played with in any such way.

How, then, are we to learn God's will in cases of this kind? Will God show us the pattern for our life in all these and like cases? Yes; no one need ever take a step in the dark. He does not show us all our life-course in one pattern; but he will let us know our duty—as we go on, step by step. If we do God's will as it is made known to us—we shall never lack knowledge of it. For example, in the matter of *promotion* in business or in any place of duty or responsibility, it is a question if one should ever seek it for himself. Let him do his duty in the position in which he is placed; let him do it faithfully, diligently, with ever increasing perfectness—but with no scheming for a higher place. In General Grant's autobiography there is this suggestive statement: "I never dared seek promotion. I was afraid if I sought it, I might get into positions which responsibilities I could not fill. I preferred to take promotion as it came to me, providentially." If this rule were followed by all, there would be fewer wrecks of great human responsibilities. God will guide us in his providence into the higher places which he wants us to fill, and the larger work he wants us to do—if only we are faithful in our present place, and wait patiently for him.

We have but one simple thing to do, if we would learn God's plan for our life. We have our present duty to do. If one is in school, his daily tasks are all he has to do. He is not to waste a moment worrying about what he will make of his life next year or in ten years. The duty of the day is the whole will of God for him. When tomorrow comes—it will be tomorrow's duty, and so on day by day. Thus he will in the end fulfill all God's will for him, by doing each little part of it as it is made known to him.

Then work must be *well done* at every point. Our hand never must slack, even for a day. Life is a great deal more serious than many of us think. Responsibility covers every moment of it. We dare not do anything carelessly. The harness-maker one day did *slack work* on a pair of lines because he was in a hurry. A few weeks later the horses attached to a family coach became frightened, and when the driver sought to hold them—the line broke and the team ran away, wrecking the carriage and badly hurting two people in it. Carelessness anywhere, for even one hour, is criminal. Besides, it is not working after the pattern. Let us learn to do every duty *well*. Let us follow the drawing to the smallest particular. Thus only can we build our life on God's plan.

Of course we are never to expect to be led and shown the way and told what to do, as if we had no brains. We have brains—and we are to use them. God gave them to us that we might think for ourselves, that we might inquire and judge and choose a plan. He guides us therefore, in many things, through our own judgment. We are to pray for light, and then think for ourselves and act—doing what seems to us to be the right thing, taking what appears to be God's way. We may sometimes make mistakes, for none of us are infallible. But we learn by making mistakes and grow wiser as we go on.

Our blessed Master in his wondrous love, has given us a work to do in this world. It matters little whether it is small or great in men's eyes; whether it is work which shall be exposed to the world's gaze, or something obscure up amid the *rafters*, in the shadows of other men's great buildings. But whatever we do—let us do it well. Let us not carve into beauty, only the part men shall see, to win human praise; while we leave the hidden parts unfinished or carelessly wrought. Let us rather work, even in the shadows, in the obscurest things, so perfectly, so beautifully, that when angels and Christ shall look down upon what we have done, they shall say, "It was love that wrought this, love for the blessed Master." Then his greeting to us will be, "Well done—good and faithful servant!"

Enlarge the Place of Your Tent

"Enlarge the place of your tent, stretch your tent curtains wide, do not hold back; lengthen your cords, strengthen your stakes." Isaiah 54:2

It is a great thing for a man to be able by his influence on others, to enrich their lives. It is said that Michael Angelo once paid a visit to the studio of Raphael, when the artist was absent. On an easel there was a canvas with the outline of a human form—beautiful—but too small. Michael Angelo took a brush and wrote under the figure the word "Amplius"—larger. The same word might be written under many lives. They may be good and beautiful—but they are too small. They need to be enlarged. They have not sufficient height or breadth.

There are many people who live in only one room, so to speak. They are intended to live in a house with many rooms: rooms of the mind, rooms of the heart, and rooms of taste, imagination, sentiment, and feeling. But these upper rooms are left unused, while they live in the basement.

A story is told of a Scotch nobleman who, when he came into possession of his estates, set about providing better houses for his people, who were living huddled together in single-roomed cottages. So he built for them pretty, comfortable houses. But in a short time each family was living as before, in one room, and renting the rest of the house. They did not know how to live in higher, better ways. The experiment taught him, that people could not be really benefitted by anything done for them merely from the outside.

Horace Bushnell put it in an epigram—"The soul of improvement—is the improvement of the soul." It is not a larger *house* which is needed for a man—but a larger *man* in the house. *A man is not made better by giving him more money, better furniture, finer pictures, richer carpets—but by giving him knowledge, wisdom, good principle, strength of character; by teaching him love.*

Some lives are narrow, by reason of the way they have let circumstances dwarf them. But we must not say that *poverty* has this effect—for many who are poor, who have to live in a little house, with few comforts and no luxuries, live a life that is large and free, as wide as the sky in its joy; while on the other hand there are those who have everything earthly that heart could desire, yet whose lives are narrow.

There are some to whom life has been so heavy a burden, that they are ready to drop by the way. They pray for health, and illness comes with its suffering and its expense. Their work is hard. They have to live in continual discomfort. Their associations are uncongenial. There seems no hope of relief. When they awake in the morning, their first consciousness is of the load they must lift and begin again to carry. Their *disheartenment* has continued so long that it has grown into *hopelessness*. The message to such is: "Enlarge the place of your tent." No matter how many or how great are the reasons for discouragement, a Christian should not let bitterness enter his heart and blind his eyes—so that he cannot see the blue sky and the shining stars.

Looked at from an earthly view-point, could any life have been more narrow in its condition than Christ's? Think who he was—the Son of God, sinless, holy, loving, and infinitely gentle of heart. Then think of the life into which he came—the relentless hatred of him, the bitter enmity which pursued him, the rejection of love which met him at every step. Think of the failure of his mission, (as it seemed), his betrayal and death. Yet he was never discouraged. He never grew bitter. How did he overcome the narrowness? The secret was love. The world hated him—but he loved on. His own received him not, rejected him—but his heart changed not toward them. Love saved him from being embittered by the narrowness. This is the one secret that will save any life from the narrowing influence of the most distressing circumstances. Widen your tent! Make room in it for Christ and for your neighbor.

There was a woman who had become embittered by a long experience of sickness, and of injustice and wrong, until she was shut up in a *prison of hopelessness*. Then, by reason of the death of a brother, a little motherless child was brought to her door. The door was opened reluctantly at first; the child was not warmly welcomed. Yet when she was received, *Christ* entered with her, and at once the dreary home began to grow brighter. The narrowness began to be enlarged. Other human needs came and were not turned away. In blessing others—the woman was blessed herself. Today there is no happier home than hers. Try it if you are discouraged. Begin to serve those who need your love and ministry. Encourage some other disheartened one—and your own discouragement will pass away. Brighten another's lonely lot—and your own will be brightened.

Some lives are made narrow by their *limitations*. Men seem not to have the same chance that others have. They may be physically incapacitated for holding their place in the *march of life*. Or they may have failed in business after many years of hard toil, and may lack the courage to begin again. They may have been hurt by folly or sin, and not seem able to take the flights they used to take. There are some people in every community who, for one cause or another, do not seem to have a chance to make much of their life. But whatever it may be which shuts one in a narrow environment, as in a little tent, the gospel of Christ brings a message of hope and cheer. Its call ever is, "Enlarge the place of your tent, stretch your tent curtains wide."

There is danger that some of us overdo our contentment. We regard as an impassable wall, certain obstacles and hindrances which God meant to be, to us, only inspirers of courage. Difficulties are not intended to stop our efforts—but to arouse us to our best. We give up too easily. We conclude that we cannot do certain things, and think we are submitting to God's will in giving up without trying to overcome, when in fact we are only showing our laziness. We suppose that our limitations are part of God's plan for us, and that we have only to accept them and make the best of them. In some cases this is true—there are barriers that are impassable—but in many cases God wants us to gain the victory over the limitations. The call ever is, "Enlarge the place of your tent!"

If there can be no *physical* victory over physical handicaps, there can always at least be a *mental* victory. We should never accept of captivity, which shuts our soul in any prison. Our spirit may be free, though our bodily life is shut up in a prison of circumstances. An English writer tells of two birds, caught and put into cages side by side. The *starling* began to resist and struggle, flying against the wires of its cage in vain efforts to escape. The *canary* accepted its captivity, and flying up on a bar, began to sing, filling all the place about with glad songs. The former bird was a captive indeed, shut up in a narrow, hopeless prison. The other turned its captivity into widest liberty and its narrow cage into a palace of victory. We say the starling acted very foolishly, and that the canary showed true wisdom. Which course do we take when we find ourselves shut up in any narrow, imprisoned life?

Life should never *cease* to widen. People talk about the "dead line"—it used to be fifty years; now it probably is less. After crossing that line, they tell us, a man cannot do his best. It is not true—at least it should not be true. A man ought to be at his best during the *last years* of his life. He ought always to be *enlarging the place of his tent* until its curtains are finally pushed out into the limitless spaces of immortality!

Help for the Common Days

Every true Christian should desire to be Christlike in character. It is not enough to be honest, and upright, and true, and just. In Christ, these strong qualities were marked--but He was also gentle, and kind, and loving, and patient. If we would be like our Master--we must have these traits of character also in us. When we pray that the beauty of the Lord may be upon us, we must ask for these finer features of His beauty--as well as for the more rugged ones. We need His strength and truth and faithfulness and justice--but we need His love and tenderness as well. And these are among the fruits of the Spirit-filled life.

"Alice is not pretty," said one of her friends, trying to define her character, "and I never heard anybody call her brilliant. But you couldn't put her anywhere—in the poorest, narrowest place—without finding in a little while that things had begun to grow about her. She could make a home in the desert, and not only would it be a home, with all the warm, welcoming feeling of one—but there would be fine, invisible lines stretching out from it to the world in every direction. I cannot imagine her in so bare a place, that she could not find joy in it; nor in so lonely a place, that the sorrowing and troubled would not find their way to her door. She has a gift for living—that's the secret."

That is the way the Spirit works in the heart in which he dwells. He opens a well of heavenly love there and its waters make the life into a garden of God. The beauty in us changes us from glory to glory, until all the grace and beauty of Christ are in us. Not to admit this heavenly Guest—is to be without God. To have him in our hearts—is to be children of God.

The influence of the indwelling Spirit is not shown merely in holy emotions, ecstatic raptures—but in most practical ways in everyday life. To be kind and charitable, to give bread to the hungry and to sacrifice a pleasure to help another over a hard place, are better evidences of the indwelling of the Spirit than any amount of effervescent talk about consecration, in a prayer meeting. To be honest on Monday, to keep a house beautiful on Tuesday, to pay one's debts on Wednesday, "to kiss a bumped forehead" on Thursday, is worth more as proof of the indwelling Spirit, than a whole hour's rapturous experience on Sunday, which *ends* with the day. God in us, means God in all our common life.

The Spirit in us gives us power for service. The apostles were bidden to tarry at Jerusalem until they were clothed with power from on high, before they would go out to preach. The world was perishing and the redemption was ready—but the messengers could not deliver their message effectively, until the Spirit had filled their hearts. We should note well this condition of power. We talk about organization, about machinery, about the church and its institutions. All this is important—but the essential power after all, is the Spirit of God. At the opening of a Methodist General Conference the bishop in charge prayed: "We thank you that we have *machinery*. Fill it with *divine power*." We must have good workers—but the best workers can do nothing unless the Spirit of God works in them.

It is a beautiful illustration of this truth which Bishop Brooks gave: "Look at the artist's chisel. Most certainly it carves the statue. The artist cannot carve without his chisel. Yet imagine the chisel, conscious that it was made to carve and that that is its function, trying to carve alone. It lays itself against the hard marble—but it has neither strength nor skill; it has no force to drive itself in; and if it had, it does not know which way it ought to go. Then we can imagine the chisel full of disappointment. 'Why cannot I carve?' it cries. Then the artist comes and seizes it. The chisel lays itself into his hand, and is obedient to him. That obedience is faith. It opens the channels between the sculptor's brain and the hard steel, and thought, feeling, imagination, skill flow down from the deep chambers of the artist's soul to the chisel's edge. The sculptor and the chisel are not two—but one. It is the unit which they make, which carves the statue."

We are but the *chisels* to carve God's statues in this world. Unquestionably we must do the work. Our *hands* must touch men's lives and bless them. Our *lips* must speak the words of life by which sinners shall be convicted, the penitent pointed to the Lamb of God, the sorrowing comforted, the discouraged heartened. *The mother, the teacher, the friend, must carve the soul of the child into the beauty of Christ.* But the chisel alone can do nothing. The artist must hold it. We must lay ourselves into the hand of the Divine Spirit, that his power, his wisdom, his grace and love may flow through us.

Our danger always is that we may fail to recognize the necessity of the Spirit in our work. We think that we can help people, that we can change bad lives into good, that we can comfort sorrow, and that we can put touches of beauty upon human souls. One fact is that *we can do nothing alone.* Then the other fact is that *we can do all these things if we are clothed with the power of the Holy Spirit.* Without the Spirit we cannot do them. The Spirit will not do them without us. These blessed and beautiful ministries can be wrought, only when we are filled with the Spirit—and the Spirit works in us and through us.

So we must yield our lives to the Spirit and to guard most carefully that nothing is ever allowed to hinder or obstruct the Spirit's working in us. It is not easy to let God into our lives. We naturally love this world, and it is easier for us to yield ourselves to the spirit of the *world* than to the Spirit of *God.* Too many yield their hearts to the Divine Guest on Sunday, and then on Monday let in again the old worldly guests who drive out the Holy Spirit.

We all know how easy it is to lose out of our hearts—the gentle thoughts and holy desires which come to us in life's quiet, sacred moments. We sit down with our bible in the pure, sweet morning, and as we read the Master's words it seems as if angels from heaven had come into our heart. We hear words of love. Desires kindled by the love of God warm our heart. As we read and pray and meditate, it is as if we were sitting in the gate of heaven and hearing the songs of the holy beings inside. But half an hour later, we must go out into the world, where a thousand other voices will break upon our ears—voices of temptation, voices of pleasure, voices of care, the calls of business, of friendship, of ambition—not all holy voices; many of them calling us away from God. How shall we carry with us all the day through all these distractions and all these allurements—the holy thoughts and feelings and desires of the morning watch?

The spirit of the *world* is fatal to the stay of the heavenly Spirit in a heart. The world is very subtle. We try to make it seem harmless—that we may keep it in our hearts. We need to ask our friends to pray for us no more greatly at any time—than when we are *prospering* in worldly ways. It is no easy task to keep our hearts filled with the Spirit of God, while we are busy all the time with the world's affairs.

If we would keep the Spirit always in our heart, we must make our heart's life heaven-like. We must live ever near to Christ, doing always the things which please him. One of the special days in the calendar of many Christians is Whitsunday—White Sunday, because anciently it was the custom for many Christian to wear white garments in toke of their purity. Let every Sunday, and every week-day, too, be a time for putting on the white robes of righteousness, as is befitting those who have received the Holy Spirit. Always we must wear these same white robes; down into the city streets, back to our work. We need to guard our white garments with most gentle care—that we get no stain or soiling on them.

It is no wonder that gentle spirits sometimes shrink from going away to meet the world's dangers. "I send you forth as *lambs* among *wolves*," said the Master. But if we keep the Spirit in our hearts, there will be no danger. Our safety lies in having this blessed Guest always in our hearts!

The Beautifying of Imperfect Living

Men have written '*lives of Jesus*', setting forth the beauty, the grace, the wisdom, the gentleness, and the power of him who was the chief among ten thousand, the altogether lovely one. In the New Testament we have *four lives of Jesus*—we call them the four gospels. But Paul tells us that in every Christian's life—the life of Jesus is to be written—"That the life of Jesus may be manifested in our mortal flesh." 2 Corinthians 4:9. And it is these lives of Christ, written in men's daily lives—which are needed to save the world.

How is the *life of Jesus* to be manifested in his followers? It is not enough to *talk* about him. There are those who, with silver tongue, can speak of Jesus eloquently and winsomely, in whom it cannot be said that his life is manifested in them. When the apostles were sent out, they were not to witness for Jesus—but were to be witnesses for him, unto him. In this sense—it is not more *preaching* which is needed today to advance the kingdom of God among men—it is more gospels in the lives of Christians. It is not what we *tell* people about Christ, which makes his name glorious in their eyes, which makes them want to know him, which draws them with their needs, their heart-hungers, their sorrows, their defeats, and failures to him. It is only what we manifest of Christ in our own life that is really witnessing for him. We preach just as much gospel—as we get into disposition, character, act, life.

What was secret of the life of Christ? You have read your New Testament and have been charmed by the matchless beauty of that life which is portrayed in the gospels. His great central feature was love--love full of compassion; love serving even to the humblest needs and at the greatest cost; love which was patient, forgiving, thoughtful, gentle; love unto the uttermost--which went to a cross to save sinners!

It was indeed a wonderful life. The half of its blessed meaning has not yet been discovered, even after nineteen centuries of scholarly study and research and of precious Christian experience. Every page reveals some new beauty in the character of Jesus, and uncovers some new depth of his love. And the qualities of that blessed life—are to shine in *our* life! His disposition, His spirit, His compassion, His patience, His meekness, His peace, His joy, His humility—these are to reappear in us! It is not enough--let us again and again remind ourselves--to preach about these gracious things in Jesus, to talk about them in our conferences, to extol them in our hymns--they must be manifested in our life! We must repeat in our own dispositions and lives--the story of Christ!

People sometimes wish they had lived in Palestine when Jesus was living there, that they could have seen his face and heard his words and received his touch and been blessed by his love. They ought to see all this in us Christians—that the life of Jesus should be manifested in us so that all who know us shall see Jesus.

Let us not forget that the cross is the truest symbol of the life of Jesus. When we think of being like him we are apt to gather out a few gentle qualities and let these make up our conception of Christ-likeness. True, he was a kindly man, a patient man, a quiet man; he was thoughtful, compassionate, unselfish, and loving.

But we must not fail to think of the *life* of Jesus, as well as of his *character*. Right here we have the other part of the picture. "Always bearing about in the body the *dying* of Jesus—that the life also of Jesus may be manifested in our body." "We who live are always delivered unto death for Jesus' sake." Here we have the strenuous aspect, the costly side.

An artist was trying to improve on a dead mother's portrait. He wanted to take out the lines. But the woman's son said, "No, no; don't take out the lines; just leave them, every one. It wouldn't be my mother, if all the lines were gone." It was well enough, he said, for young people who never had known a care, to have faces with no wrinkles; but when one has lived seventy years of love and serving and self-denial, it would be like lying to cover up their track.

He did not want a picture with the sacred story of all the mother's toil and pain and tears, taken out of the face. Likewise, no picture of Jesus is true which has only the lovely graces, and leave out the marks of pain and sorrow and struggle. His visage was marred. There were marks of thorns on his brow. His hands were most gentle and helpful—but now in heaven there are prints of nails in them. It would be false to paint the picture of Jesus, and leave out the marks which sorrow and pain ploughed in his face. Ah, it was at infinite cost that Jesus redeemed us!

If we would be like Christ, therefore, we must be like him in serving even to the uttermost. We must not merely tell people how Christ loved men—we must *manifest* the love of Christ for men in our own life. We must not merely point them to an historic cross, standing on Calvary, far back in the centuries—they must see the cross, right before their eyes, in *our* life!

Too many of us seem content to have the hope of being like Jesus merely for far-away future. We appear to have little thought or desire or expectation of a present likeness to Jesus. But it is in our own mortal flesh that this life of Jesus is to be manifested. It is here and now that we are to show the world, in our own love and service, how Jesus loved and served. Of course we shall wear the full beauty of holiness in heaven; but it is here, amid temptation and struggle, that Christ wants us to be his witnesses—holy in the midst of unholiness; in the world—but living heaven's life; amid need and sorrow and poverty—but ever helping, serving, relieving. No doubt Christ loved the world and gave himself for it—nineteen centuries ago; but now we are the body of Christ, and we must love the world and give ourselves for it. In no other way can the life of Jesus be truly manifested in our mortal flesh.

There are those who say it is impossible to repeat the life of Jesus in our life. He was the perfect man—the one perfect man in all the ages—and we are imperfect, fallen, and sinful. He was the Son of God—God manifest in the flesh, and we are children of earth. We cannot be like Jesus in holiness and beauty. We cannot live as he lived, pouring out love like his. God does tell us that we are to manifest the life of Jesus in our mortal flesh. The meaning is that the blessed life will manifest itself in us, if only we will yield ourself to it, that it may fill us and possess us. Christ himself lives again—in every one of his true followers.

Poor indeed may be the best of our striving to live Christ's life, to manifest the life of Jesus in our body. But if we are sincere in our endeavor, if our heart is truly yielded up to Christ, he will enter into us and live out his own blessed life in us. Then our imperfect living will be made beautiful in God's sight, and the world will be impressed with the shining of the face of Jesus which it sees in us!

Are the Beautiful Things True?

In a private letter from a professing Christian, is this eager longing: "For the last month or more I have been drifting away from God, and have not been able to drop anchor. The more I read and study the life of Jesus, the farther I seem to drift. I find myself asking the question continually, 'Are all these things true? They certainly are beautiful to read about—but are they true?'"

We say that God does not manifest himself to us; yet he does reveal himself far more actually than we think. There is a picture of Augustine and his mother which represents them looking up to heaven with deep longing and great eagerness, as if listening for something. One is says, "If God would only speak to us!" and the other replies, "Perhaps he is speaking to us now, and we do not hear him!"

Philip said, "Lord, show us the Father," and Jesus replied, "Have I been so long time with you, and do you not know me, Philip? He who has seen me has seen the Father." Philip thought he had never seen the Father, and Jesus told him he had been seeing the Father for three years. What Philip had in mind was some revealing of visible glory, some outshining of majesty and splendor, a transfiguration—that was the way he thought God must appear. When Jesus said, "He who has seen me has seen the Father," he referred to his daily life with his disciples. The very purpose of the Incarnation was to show God to men, in a common, everyday human life which they could understand. Jesus was showing God to men when he was patient with their dullness, gentle with their faults, longsuffering and merciful with their sins, compassionate toward their sorrows. We see God continually in the same familiar ways. A writer says that most men are religious when they look upon the faces of their dead babies. The materialism which at other times infects them with doubts of immortality, drops away from them in this holy hour.

People say, "If we could see miracles we would believe." But it was not miracles to which Jesus referred in his own life, when he said that he had been revealing the Father all the time he had been with the disciples. He referred to the kindnesses he had shown, and the gentle things he had continually done in his associations with the people in the common life of his everyday.

Have you really never seen God? If you think of God as only burning majesty, shining glory, you will say, "No, I never saw God." But the splendor of Sinai clouds and flaming fire, is not God—God is love. You have seen God a thousand times in love, in peace, in goodness. You have seen him in daily providential care, in the sweet things of your home, in sacred friendships, and in countless revealings of goodness. Think how you have been blessed all your life in many ways. Do not call it *chance*, or *luck*—there is no such thing.

A heart-hungry girl asked, "Why has no one ever seen God?" Yet she herself had seen God every day, every hour of her life, in the goodness and mercy which had followed her from her infancy. Say not any more, "I have never seen God." You were in danger, and a mysterious protection preserved you from harm. You had a great sorrow which you thought you could not possibly endure, and there came a sweet comfort which filled your heart with peace. There was a strange tangle of affairs which seemed about to wreck everything in your life and it was all straightened out as by invisible hands, in a way you never dreamed of. You had a crushing loss, which seemed about to overwhelm you, and lo! The loss proved a gain. You were wrongly treated by a pretended friend, and the stars all seemed to have gone out of your sky. Today you are quietly praising God for it all, for it delivered you from what would have been a great misfortune, and gave you instead a true friendship, and a rich happiness which fills all your life. You had a painful sickness which shut you away in the darkness for weeks, and you thought it a grievous experience. Today you thank God for it, for you learned new lessons in the darkness. All your years have been full of remarkable deliverances, strange guidance, gentle comforts, answered prayers, sweet friendships, divine love and care. Yet you say you have never seen God, and you ask, "How may I know that the beautiful things which the New Testament tells me about Christ are true?"

How may we learn the reality of spiritual things? Only by *experience*. In one of the Psalms it is said: "those who know your name, will put their trust in you." And "name" in the Bible means personality, the person himself. Human friendships are formed in experience. We meet one we have never seen before. Little by little we learn to know him, finding in him qualities that please us, and coming at length to love and trust him as a friend. In the same way only can we learn to know and love God. We read of his goodness, his justice, his truth, his loving-kindness, his faithfulness. But we must come into personal relations with him, before we can know that these qualities are in him. We can learn to know him only in experience.

The story of Lady Aberdeen's conversion to Christ is very suggestive. She was long in doubt—wavering, indecisive, not knowing what to do. In her perplexity she sat one day under a tree in her garden, in deep thought. She had been asking the question, "How can I know that these things are true? Is Christ real?" She could not be sure. "Act as if I were true," said a mystic voice, "and you will find that I am." Nothing could have been more reasonable. She did not stop to ask whether the voice she heard was divine, or only an impression. To her it was the voice of Christ, and he was bidding her to try him. "You do not know whether I am or not. Act as if I were. I offer you life, rest, joy, peace; you do not know whether there are such blessings or not. Act as if there were. Test me. Test my words." She did so, and she was not disappointed.

How do we know that any of these invisible things are true? How do we know that there is any God? We need not seek proofs that there is a God; the Bible offers none. When Philip asked, "Lord, show us the Father," Jesus replied, "He who has seen me, has seen the Father." In Jesus Christ, therefore we see God. Look at Christ and you will see God.

Let no one think that God wants to hide himself, wants to be only dimly, obscurely seen. He wants his friendship with us to be real and close. He does not want us to walk in darkness, to grope in gloom. He does not want to be unreal to us. He wants us to know him as we know no other friend. He wants prayer to be as real to us as talk with any human friend. Yet we say, "These things are very beautiful—but are they true?" Yes, they are the realest things in the world. How shall we then make them real to our experience? Christ is real—he is our Savior, our Master, and our Friend. Someone asked, "How can I learn to love Christ more?" "Trust him more," was the answer. "How can I trust him more?" "Love him more." Loving and trusting go together. The more you love him the more you will trust him, and the more will you find in him to love. The best, the truest, the most faithful human friend will disappoint you some time, in something; but Christ, never.

The *New* Kind of Love

Why should Jesus have called his commandment of love a *new* commandment? There was an old commandment that ran, "You shall love your neighbor as yourself." Some people suppose that this is the same as the commandment that Jesus gave to his disciples. But there are two differences. The old commandment referred to your neighbor—that is, to everybody; the new refers to your brother, your fellow-Christian. The other difference is in the *measure* of the love—"as yourself"; "as I have loved you."

The world never knew what love meant, until Jesus came and lived among men. "As yourself" —this puts self and others side by side; "as I have loved you" —this carries us away beyond that, for Jesus made sacrifice of himself in loving his disciples.

And so this touches our lives at very practical points. "Love is patient, and is kind." The trouble with too many of us is that our kindness is spasmodic, is shown only when we feel like it, and is checked continually by things which happen. But nothing ever stopped the flow of Christ's kindness; nothing ever should check the flow of a Christian's kindness.

"Love… does not behave itself unseemly." That is, it never forgets itself, is never crude. All uncharitableness is unseemly. Nothing is more remarkable in the story of Christ's life, than his unfailing respect for people. He seemed to have almost reverence for everyone that came before him, even the poorest, the lowest, and the worst. The reasons were, that he loved everyone, and that he saw in each the glorious possibilities of heavenly sonship. If we had our Master's lofty regard for, and his deep interest in, the lives of men, we would never act in an unseemly way toward even the unworthiest. The poet said he would never have for his friend, that man who would needlessly set his foot upon a worm. If it befits us to treat considerately, a mere worm—how should we treat even the poorest, the lowliest, who wears the divine image, and is "but little lower than God"?

"Love is not provoked." That is, it does not become vexed or irritated at what another may say or do. Yet many people seem to overlook this line of the picture. Nothing is more common that ill-temper. Some people get provoked even at things. A boy the other day flew into a rage at his bicycle from which he had fallen, and beat the machine unmercifully. A man stumbled over a chair, and in a violet passion kicked the chair all about the room. No other infirmity is so often confessed as bad temper. Many people will tell you that they find no other fault in themselves so hard to overcome. Nor do they seem ashamed to make the confession; apparently they do not consider the fault a serious one. They speak of it apologetically, as an infirmity of nature, a family failing, a matter of temperament, certainly not a fault to be taken seriously. Bad temper has been called the vice of the virtuous. Men and women whose characters are noble, whose lives are beautiful in every other way, have this one fault—they are sensitive, touchy, easily ruffled, easily hurt.

But we make a grave mistake when we let ourselves think that ill temper is merely a trifling weakness. It is a disfiguring blemish. Jesus set for us the perfect model of living, and he was never provoked. In all his experience of persecution, wrong, mocking, and injustice—he was not once provoked. He would have us live the same life. When he bids us love one another as he has loved us—this is part of what he means.

Loving one another as Christ loves us, makes it easier for others to live and work with us. A minister tells of some people in his church who are excellent workers, full of zeal and energy—but he says they will not drive double. There are horses of this kind; they will not pull in a team—but have to be driven single. So it seems there are people who have the same infirmity. They want to do good—but they cannot work with others. There is a kind of carriage which has only two wheels and a seat for one. It is suggestively called a *sulky*, because the rider rides alone. Some people seem happiest when they ride alone.

The love of Christ teaches a better way. We need to learn to think of others, those with whom we are united in Christian life and work. It is so in all associated life. It is so in *marriage*. When two lives are brought together in close relation, after having lived separately, it is evident that both cannot have their own way in everything. There is not room for any two people to have their own way in the marriage relation. They are now one, occupying only the place of one, and they must live as one. There must be either the entire displacement of one by the other, the losing of the individuality of one in that of the other, the entire giving up of one to the other—or else there must be the mutual blending of the one in the other. Love unites them, and they are no longer twain—but one.

The same principle must prevail in Christian life and work. Headstrong individualism must be softened and modified by love. Jesus sent forth his disciples by *two by two*. Two working together, are better than two working separately. One is strong in one point and weak in another; the second is strong where the first is weak, and thus the two supplement each other. Paul speaks of certain Christians as yoke-fellows. Yoke-fellows draw together patiently and steadily, two necks under the same yoke, two hearts pouring their love and fellowship into one service.

We know the importance in Christian life, of being pleasant to live with and work with. It never should have to be said of us that other people cannot work with us. The secret of being agreeable yoke-fellows, is *love*. This means self-losing, self-forgetfulness. The Christian who is always wanting to have positions of prominence, to be chairman or president, first in something, has not caught the spirit of the love of Christ, who came not to be ministered unto—but to minister. Love never demands the first place—it works just as enthusiastically and as faithfully at the *foot* of a committee, as at the *head* of it. It is content to be overlooked, set aside—if only Christ is exalted. It is patient with the faults of fellow-workers.

We are called to a love like Christ's, in building up his kingdom.
He *loved* and *gave* himself; we must love and give ourselves. We can serve Christ and our fellow men, only in a sacrificial service. "As I have loved you" means loving to the uttermost.

This is a love which is not affected by the character, or the past life of the person we love. To love as Christ loved—is to love the worst, the least worthy; to love them until they are lifted up, cleansed and transfigured. To love as Christ loved—is to let his love into our own lives, to learn to live as he lived—in gentleness, in patience, in humility, in kindness, in endurance, in all sweetness of spirit, in all helpfulness and self-denial. It is not easy; but it was not easy for Christ to love as he did.

The trouble with too much of what we call *love*—is that it costs nothing, is only a sort of gilded selfishness, is not ready to sacrifice anything, to give up, to suffer, or to endure. Let us not profane the holy name of love, by calling such life as this love. To love as Christ loves, is to repeat Christ's sacrifice continually, in serving, in forgiving, bearing, enduring, that others may be helped, blessed and saved.

As I Have Loved You

The *art of living together* is not easily learned. Indeed, it is the one lesson of life— and it takes all life to learn it. We cannot evade the lesson, for we cannot live apart. We are not made for solitariness. We need continual contact with others, in order that we may have the benefit of the impact and discipline of life on life. We are made to love together, and the ideal is very high. Christ gave the secret to his disciples. They were to *love one another*, and the *measure* of their love should be, "As I have loved you."

When we have learned to live in this way, we shall have no trouble in living together. It is worth our while to study the Master's rule of love, that we may know how to make it our own. How did he love his disciples? We have it in his *every-day life* with his disciples.

In the broadest sense his love was unselfish. SELF never thrust itself into any thought of his. It is selfishness which so often mars men's treatment of each other. "How will this affect me?" is the question which rises first in deciding what to do. It never rose at all in Christ's dealing with others. He thought only and always of what he could do to give pleasure or do good.

The spirit of unselfishness showed itself first of all, in *unvarying kindness*. His heart was sensitive to every pain or suffering in any life. He was touched with the feeling of every human infirmity, and longed to help or strengthen or comfort. He was ever ready to do gentle or obliging things. He did not expect others to help or serve him—he came not to be ministered unto—but to minister.

We cannot love as he loved, in the great infinite ways of his divine power. We cannot imitate his miracles of mercy and helpfulness. We cannot feed multitudes with our little loaves and fishes, or go along the streets and heal sick people by hundreds. But for every miracle that Jesus wrought, he did a thousand simple deeds of kindness, just such deeds as we can do. "As I have loved you" means therefore no impossible thing in our daily life. The divinest thing in the world is love shown in *unselfish kindness*. It may be only a gentle word, the commonest act of helpfulness to a lowly one, a bit of cheer to one who is discouraged. We cannot know the power of helpfulness there is in the *commonest kindnesses* we may do.

The love of Christ was always *patient*. Impatience mars a great deal of human love—but he never showed the slightest impatience to anyone. He did not fly into a temper as we do so often when people try us. His disciples were dull and slow learners. It seemed as if they never would learn the lessons he wanted to teach them. But he did not chide them. A great teacher said he never could forget how a boy whom he had rebuked for his dullness in not understanding some lesson, looked into his face and said, "Indeed, sir, I am doing the best I can!" The teacher said it shamed him to think how he had wronged and hurt the boy by his impatient and unworthy outbreak. Jesus never did anything like that. He had infinite patience with the slowest scholar he was trying to teach.

He had patience also with his disciples in their many failures in faithfulness and obedience. We are very exacting in our friendships; making large demands upon those we call friends, impatient even of the slightest lack of devotion; quick to resent any lack in loyalty or service. But Jesus bore with his friends in all their lack of faithfulness, never rebuking them and never withdrawing the rich grace of his love from them. They slept, when he had asked them to watch beside him while he was enduring his agony. Their failure grieved him sorely—but he uttered no word of complaint or chiding. It hurt him to have them so misunderstand his teaching about himself—but the only word he spoke was, "Have I been so long time with you—and have you not known me?" He was patient with their faults, their failures, their fears, their doubts, their denials, and all their unfaithfulness. They made friendship very hard for him—but he never failed nor faltered in his loving—he loved them unto the end.

Think what it would mean if we were to live together in this patient and forbearing way as Christians. Is not impatience one of the faults in our ordinary fellowship, which do most to mar the perfectness of our relations as Christians? Do we not too easily grow weary of the dullness of those we ought to help? Do we not chafe at the slowness of those who are walking with us? Do we not fail continually in sympathy with those who are weak and faint, with those who are feeble in body or mind? Do we not show irritation when others misunderstand us, when one doubts the sincerity and the reality of our friendship, or when those who we have trusted prove unworthy of our confidence? No doubt there are sore testing of love—but remember what "As I have loved you" means to us. The law of love is not "Do to others— what they have done to you," but "Do to them—what you would have them do to you."

Few of us go through life without being unjustly treated. The teacher was wise who exhorted those he taught, to accustom themselves to injustice. It is not an easy lesson to learn—but it is part of "As I have loved you." We must keep our love sweet, patient, forgiving, bearing all injury and wrong, if we would obey the Master's word and follow his example.

"As I have loved you." How small and inadequate much of our loving of each other is, when we lay it alongside this pattern! Christ loved men because he was their Friend. He never asked whether they were worthy or unworthy. He despised no one—but saw in every meanest wreck of life—a possible child of God and sought to lift the unworthiest to glory. In living together as Christians, we are to love all whom Christ loves. Not everyone is beautiful, holy, or a saint—but love makes us gentle with rudeness, harshness, or unkindness; patient with faultiness, pitiful toward weakness. Whatever others may do to us or fail to do—we must always love them.

F.W. Robertson tells of a friend who had failed to speak a word for him when he was falsely charged, leaving him defenseless against a slander. But he did not complain. He only says, "How rare it is to have a friend who will defend you thoroughly and boldly!" Yet that is what a friend should do. If you hear a word spoken against your friend, your fellow-Christian, if you love him as Christ loves you—you will defend him, stand between him and the false thing charged against him. That is the way the Master did, when any of his disciples were maligned. We cannot be too ready to speak for others, when they are criticized or calumniated. Too often we forget this requirement of Christian love. Some even seem to be glad to hear evil of others, and to believe it, and to allow suspicion to poison their friendship. This is cowardly, as well as unchristian. The true course regarding evil spoken of others, if possible, is to refuse to *hear* it; if we must hear it, to refuse to *believe* it; if it is so plain that we cannot but believe it, then to cast the *mantle of charity* over it and seek in every way to save the person against whom the evil is proved. "If any man is overtaken in any fault, you who are spiritual, restore such a one in a spirit of gentleness; looking to yourself, lest you also be tempted." That is loving as Christ loves us.

Is Christ-love the master-passion of our life?

Divine Use of Human Cooperation

The human part in grace is always important. A study of our Lord's miracles illustrates this. The divine power was imparted, usually, through human cooperation. For example, the man with the withered hand was bidden to stretch forth his hand. This was precisely what the man could not do, and had not been able to do for many years. Yet if he was to receive the healing, this was the way it was to come to him. Had he replied that obedience to the command was impossible; his arm might not have been restored. This would have been unbelief in him. But he instantly made the effort to obey, thus magnifying faith; and as he tried to stretch forth the withered hand, the divine power was exerted, and his arm was restored to strength.

Ten lepers, huddled together in their camp, cried to Jesus, as they saw him passing by, imploring him to have mercy upon them. His compassion was stirred at sight of their abject misery—but him manner of answering their pleading, seemed remarkable. He bade them go and show themselves to the priests. This was what the law required a cleansed leper to do in order to receive a certificate of healing, that he might be admitted back into society. There would be no use in their showing themselves to the priests while they were still lepers. So they might have said, waiting to be cleansed before starting toward the priests. But if they had done this they might never have been healed. The cure of their disease, though wrought by Jesus, was to come to them through their own faith, and their faith must show itself in obedience. The men seem to have asked no questions. They took the bidding of the great Healer as an answer to their beseeching, implying an assurance that when they had come to the priests they would find themselves cleansed. So they set out at once, and eagerly, on their journey.

Very strikingly runs the record: "As they went—they were cleansed." The healing was divine—but it was dependent upon human cooperation. If the men had not gone on their way, the cure might never have been wrought. As they believed and obeyed—the healing of Christ swept through them, and their flesh came again as the flesh of a little child.

These illustrations suggest a law of the divine working which is general in its application. Divine grace does not act in a life or through a life independently of the person's own consent and cooperation. It stands at the door and knocks—but it never lifts the latch nor forces an entrance; he who is within must rise and open the door. It is ready to impart strength and new life—but there is something for us to do before the divine power will become efficient. We may be as utterly unable to do the thing which is commanded, as was the man with the withered arm to obey the Master's bidding—but, like him, we must assent in our heart, and must exert our will in the effort to obey. The *doing* of the impossible thing is not ours—but the *willing* to obey is ours. If we say we cannot do it, we are showing unbelief.

Some people think that it is the part of humility, to confess weakness and inability in the presence of divine commands. They suppose that God is pleased with such lowliness of spirit. But this is not humility, it is unbelief, and God is never pleased with unbelief. He is never so unreasonable as to give us any command we cannot obey, for with the divine bidding is included also and always, divine power sufficient to enable us to obey. "Command what you will—and give what you command," was an ancient prayer of faith which was not presumptuous. Paul understood it when he said, "I can do all things, through Christ who strengthens me."

Yet there is a vast amount of failure just at this point in human experience. Men hear the divine bidding, and they understand vaguely, at least, that they ought to obey. But they suppose that they must wait for the power before they can obey, and get the blessing. So they sit down in what seems to them the attitude of faith, expecting to receive an inflowing of grace to enable them to do that which they desire to do. But the grace does not come. The mistake they make, is in not instantly willing to do the will of God. If they would assent to the divine command, and attempt to stretch forth their withered hand to do the Lord's work—the hand would become living and strong.

Countless Christian people never do anything worth while for Christ, because they think they cannot do anything. They say they have no ability, no skill, no training, for service. Really, however, they need only to begin to do the duties which come to their hand day by day; if they would will to make the effort, power and skill would be imparted. They do, indeed, need the help of Christ—but that help is always waiting to be given if they will begin to do their part.

There are many who do not enter upon a Christian life because they are waiting for something which they think they must have first—some feeling, some experience, before they can really become Christ's disciples. They want to know that they are forgiven, or to have in them evidences that their life has been changed, before they set out to follow Christ. But they will never find the blessing they expect, until they have entered on a life of obedience, just as the lepers would not have been cleansed, if they had not started on the way to the priest. Those who hear Christ's call, and wish to be his disciples, should wait for nothing. They should begin immediately to follow him. As they go on, they will receive grace, and blessings will be given.

So it is in every phase of Christian life—the divine working waits for human assent and effort. We must keep ourselves in the attitude of obedience, quick to do whatever our Lord may command. Then, as we strive to do his will, thus showing our faith, the power of God will be imparted to us.

There is one class of our Lord's miracles, which illustrates our responsibility for the work of God in others as well as in ourselves. It is said that Jesus could do no mighty work in Nazareth—nothing more than the curing of a few sick folk—because of the people's unbelief. Thus the blessing of healing was kept from many sick and suffering ones, because men disbelieved. A father besought Jesus to cure his demoniac son—but the father's faith was imperfect. Jesus told him that, if he could believe, the cure would be wrought, implying that it would not be wrought with the father's faith weak as it then was. Thus the imperfection of the man's believing, prevented the child's restoration to sanity. When at length the father's faith became stronger, the boy was healed.

Thus on every side, this truth has most serious bearing on our life. There never can be a failure in the divine blessing—but the receiving of blessing is with us. We need to give most earnest heed to ourselves, that we may not be wanting in cooperation with the divine working, so as to miss blessing for ourselves, or to fail to be God's messenger of good to others.

Converted Tongues

The power to communicate good which God has lodged in the human tongue, is simply incalculable. It can impart knowledge; utter words which will shine like lamps in darkened hearts; speak kindly sentences which will comfort sorrow or cheer despondency; breathe thoughts which will arouse, inspire, quicken, animate heedless souls; even whisper the secret of life-giving Gospel to those who are dead. What good we could do with our tongues, if we would use them to the limit of their capacity—no human being can compute. The opportunity does not lie alone in formal speech, as in the sermon, or the lesson, or in the occasional serious talk—but it extends to all conversation, even to the most casual greeting on the street.

A godly man once wrote to some friends: "I long to see you, that I may impart unto you some spiritual gift." He knew the value of the gift of speech, and sought in every sentence he uttered to impart some help, some comfort, some warning or cheer. How it would change the current of conversation in parlor, office, shop, on the street, in the railway-car, if all Christian people were to utter only such words as would convey some spiritual blessing to those to whom they speak!

What is the staple of conversation now among average Christian? Listen for a day, and make careful note of every word you hear. How much of it is worth recording? How many sentences are spiritually helpful, calculated to kindle higher aspirations or start upward impulses? How much of it is utterly empty and idle, mere chaff that feeds no heart-hunger, inspires no energy, kindles no joy, and helps no one to live better? How much of it is careless scandal, unjust and injurious criticism of the absent? How much of it that flatters and pleases is hypocritical and insincere?

It is startling to think of what Christian conversation *might* be, and *ought* to be—and then of what it *is.* Surely this matter demands the careful attention of every Christian man and woman. Why should such a power for good be wasted? Why should our Christian development be retarded by the misuse of the marvelous gift of speech? It were infinitely better that one was born dumb, than that, having a tongue, one should use it to scatter evil and sorrow, or to sow the seeds of bitterness and pain. What is it that our Lord says about *having to give account for every idle word?* And if for the *idle* words we must give account, how much more for the words which stain, or injure, or fall as a destructive blight into other hearts!

When we give ourselves to Christ, we must give him our tongues. It was not without significance that, when the Holy Spirit came down on the day of Pentecost, the manifestation was in "tongues like as of fire." *Fire* signifies *purification.* And one of the first results of this heavenly baptism, was that the disciples began to speak with other tongues. One meaning of this certainly was that *true conversion converts the speech that a Christian must speak with a new tongue.*

We are not left without inspired instructions as to the kind of words we should speak. "Let no corrupt communication proceed out of your mouth—but that which is good to the use of edifying, that it may minister grace unto the hearers." In these words there are two features of purely Christian speech, which are enjoined. One is *purity*, absolute purity. No corrupt communication is to flow from a consecrated tongue. There is a great deal of impurity in the speech of some professors of religion. Filthy stories are repeated, and there are vile allusions and innuendoes which stain the lips that utter them, and the heart of him who hears. Christian speech should be white as snow. In familiar conversation, nothing should be uttered which would not be spoken in the presence of the most refined and honored ladies. How does our everyday speech stand this test?

Then look at the other requirement. "Let only such communication proceed out of your mouth as is good to the use of *edifying* that will minister *grace* unto the hearers." Christian speech, every sentence of it, must be such as will *edify* those who hear, and minister *grace* to them. Purity is only negative—but more is required. Each word must be fitted in some way to build up character, and add to its beauty.

Words uttered fall, and are forgotten, as their echo dies away—but they leave their mark. They either beautify or mar. They either make the life brighter or they sully it. They either build up or they tear down what before was built. A warm breath upon the mystic frost-work on the window-pane on a winter's morning, causes all its glory to vanish. So before the breath of impure speech, the soul's glory melts into ruin. The Christian's speech must edify and minister grace. On how many lips which are now garrulous with flippant words, would this test lay the finger of silence! Yet this is the rule, the standard, by which, according to the apostle, all Christian speech is to be tried.

This does not imply that only *solemn* words may be spoken. There is nothing gloomy about the religion of Christ. You look in vain through our Lord's own conversation for one gloomy sentence. He scattered only *sunshine*. But all his words were fitted to be *helpful* words. He sought to leave some gift or blessing with everyone he met. He spoke words which made the careless thoughtful, which kindled hope in despairing souls, which left lights burning where all was dark before, which comforted the sorrowing and cheered the despairing. For everyone he met, he had some message. Yet there was no cant in his speech. He did not go about with a long face, uttering his messages in sanctimonious tone and phrase. Like all his life, his speech was sunny.

He is to be our model. The *affectation of devoutness* never ministers grace. It only caricatures religion. We are not to fill our speech with solemn phrases, and deal them out to everyone we meet. Yet with Christ in our hearts we are to impart something of Christ to everyone to whom we converse.

There are a thousand ways of giving help. There are times when humor ministers grace, when the truest Christian help is to make a man laugh. Infinite are the necessities of human lives. Our feeling toward others is ever to be a strong desire to do them good. We have an errand with each one with whom we are permitted to hold even the briefest and most casual conversation. What it is, we may not know—but if the desire is in our heart, God will use us to minister blessing in some way. Opportunities for such ministry are occurring continually. In a morning's greeting we may put so much heart and so much Christ into phrase and tone, as to make our neighbor happier all the day. In a few moments' conversation by the wayside, or during the formal call, or in the midst of the day's heat and strife—we may drop the word which will lift a burden, or strengthen a fainting heart, or inspire a new hope.

"Yes, find always time to say some earnest word between the idle talk." So we may leave blessings at every step of our way. Our words in season, throbbing with love, and wafted by the breath of silent prayer, shall be medicine to every heart into which any simplest sentence of our speech may fall.

Speak It Out

No doubt there is a duty of *silence*. There are times when silence is golden. But there is also a duty of *speech*. There are times when silence is sin. There are times when it is both ungrateful and disloyal to God—not to speak of his love and goodness, or witness before men in strong, unequivocal words.

We ought to speak out the messages given us for others. God puts something into the heart of every one of his creatures, that he would have that creature utter. He puts into the *star*, a message of light; you look up into the heavens at night, and it tells you its secret. Who knows what a blessing a star may be to a weary traveler who finds his way by it, or to the sick man lying by his window, and in his sleeplessness looking up at the glimmering point of light in the calm, deep heavens? God gives to a *flower,* a message of beauty and sweetness, and for its brief life it tells out its message to all who can read it. Who can count up the good even a flower may do, as it blooms in the garden or as it is carried into a sick-room or into the cheerless chamber of poverty?

Especially does God give to every human soul a message to deliver. To one it is some revealing of science. A great astronomer spoke of himself as thinking over God's thought after him, as he traced out the paths of the stars. To the poet God gives thoughts of beauty which he is to speak to the world; and the world is richer, sweeter, and better for hearing his message. We do not realize how much we owe to the men and women who along the centuries, have given forth their songs of hope, cheer, comfort, and inspiration.

We cannot all write poems or hymns, or compose books which will bless men; but if we live near the heart of Christ, there is not one of us into whose ear he will not whisper some fragment of truth, some revealing of grace or love, or to whom he will not give some new experience of comfort in sorrow, some new glimpse of glory. Each friend of Christ, living close to him, learns something from him, and of him, which no one ever has learned before, which he is to forth tell to the world.

Each one should speak out, therefore, his own message. If it be only a single word, it will yet bless the earth. If one of the *flowers* that bloom in summer days in the fields and gardens had refused to bloom, hiding its little gift of beauty—the world would be poorer and less lovely. If but one of the myriad *stars* in the heavens had refused to shine, keeping its little beam locked in its breast—the nights would be a little darker than they are. And any human life that fails to hear its message and learn its lesson, or fails to speak it out, keeping it locked in the silence of the heart—leaves this earth a little poorer. But every life, even the lowliest, that learns of God and then speaks out its message, adds something to the world's blessing and beauty.

We ought to speak our heart's joy. There is something very strange in the tendency, which seems so common in human lives, to hide the *joy*—and tell the *misery*. Anyone who will keep an account of what people he meets say to him, will probably find that a large proportion of them will say little that is pleasant and happy, and much that is dreary and sad. They will tell him of their bodily aches, pains, and infirmities. They will complain bitterly of the *heat* if it is warm—or of the *chill* if it is cold. They will speak of the discouragements in their business, the hardships in their occupation, the troubles in their various duties, and all the manifold miseries, real or imagined, that have fallen to their lot. But they will have very little to say of their prosperities, their health, their three good meals a day, their encouragements, favors, friendships, and manifold blessings.

Yet it is of this latter class of experiences that the world ought to hear the most. There is no command in the Bible which says we should empty the tale of all our woes into people's ears. It would be far sweeter service if we were to speak only of the pleasant things. And there always is something pleasant even in the most cheerless circumstances, if only we have an eye to find it.

There is a legend that says that once Jesus and his disciples, as they journeyed, saw a dead dog lying by the wayside. The disciples showed disgust and loathing—but the Master said, "what beautiful teeth the creature has!" The legend has its lesson for us. Miss Muloch tells of a gentleman and a lady in a lumberyard, by a dirty, foul-smelling ruin. The lady said, "How good the pine boards smell!" "Pine boards!" exclaimed her companion. "Just smell this foul ruin!" "No, thank you," the lady replied; "I prefer to smell the pine boards." She was wiser than he. It is far better for us to find the sweetness that is in the air than the foulness. It is better, also, to talk to others of the smell of pine boards, than of the heavy odors of stagnant ruins.

There is a large field of opportunities for saying good to others. Many people seem too dilatory of words of encouragement. They have the kindly thoughts in their hearts—but they do not utter them. Of course, there are things in many a heart, which had better not be expressed. There are silences which are better than speech. We should never speak harsh, uncharitable, hurtful words, which will only give needless pain, break hearts, and sunder friendships, and which can never be unsaid. It is bad enough in ill-temper, to have even bitter *thoughts* of others, of our friends, of any who bear God's image—but it is far worse to let such thoughts find utterance! Then the injury done is irreparable.

But we should never fail to speak out kindly thoughts and feelings. Some people seem to think that the utterance of complimentary words, however well deserved, is weak, sentimental, and unworthy. But it is not, if the things said are sincere and altogether true. Others fail to recognize the value of cheerful, hopeful words—and do not understand that it is worth while to speak them. The truth is, however, that words of encouragement, of inspiration, of cheer—are better ofttimes than angels' visits to those to whom they are spoken. We ought not to withhold that which is in our power to give without cost, and which will so richly bless hungry hearts and weary spirits.

Your neighbor is in sorrow. It is known for days and days that a loved one is hovering between life and death. Then the crape on the door announces that death has conquered, that the home is darkened. You want to help—but you shrink from intruding upon the sorrow. With a heart full of affectionate longing to be of use— you yet do nothing. Is there no way by which your brotherly love might make your neighbor's load a little lighter or his heart a little stronger? Are we not too timid in the presence of other's sorrows? God wants us all to be true comforters. Sorrow is very sacred, and we must enter its sanctuary with reverence. But we must beware that we do not fail in affection's duty, in the hour when our brother's heart is broken. The tenderest sympathy locked up in the heart, avails no more than if our heart were cold.

Perhaps it is in our *homes* that the lesson is most needed. There is a great deal of sweet love there, which never finds expression. We keep sad silences ofttimes with those who are dearest to us, even when their hearts are crying out for sympathetic words. In many homes that lack rich and deep happiness, it is not more love that is needed—but the flowing out of the love in little words, acts, and expressions. A husband loves his wife, and would give his life for her; but there are days and days that he never tells her so, nor reveals the sweet truth to her by any sign or token. The wife loves her husband with warm, faithful affection; but she has fallen into the habit of making no demonstration, saying nothing about her love; going through the home life almost as if there were no love in her heart. No wonder husbands and wives drift apart in such homes. *Hearts*, too, need their daily bread, and starve and die if it is withheld from them.

There are parents who make the same mistake with their children. They love them—but they do not reveal their love. They allow it to be taken for granted. After infancy passes, they quietly drop out of their fellowship with their children—all tenderness, all caresses and marks of fondness. On the first intimation of danger of any kind, their love reveals itself in anxious solicitude and prompt efforts to help— but in the daily life of the home, there is no show of tenderness. The love is unquestioned—but, like the vase of ointment unbroken, it sends out no perfume. The home life may be free from all bitterness, all that is unloving and unkind—and yet it has sore lack. It is not in what is *done* that the secret of the lack of happiness must be sought—but in what is not done.

It is not enough to love—the love must find *expression*. We must do it, too, before it is too late. Some people wait until the need is past, and then come up with their laggard sympathy. When the neighbor is well again, they call to say how sorry they are he has been so sick. Would not a kindly inquiry at the door, or a few flowers sent to his room where he was ill, have been a fitter and more adequate expression of brotherly interest? When a man without their help has gotten through his long battle with business difficulties or embarrassments, and is well on his feet again—then they come with their congratulations. Would it not have been better if they had proved their care for him in some way when he needed strong practical sympathy? The time to show our friendship is when our friend is under the shadow of enmity, when evil tongues misrepresent him—and not when he has gotten vindication and stands honored.

There are those, too, who wait until death has come, before they begin to speak their words of appreciation and commendation. There are many who say their first truly generous words of others, beside their coffins. They bring their flowers then, although they never gave a flower when their friends were living. Many a person goes down in defeat, under life's burdens, unhelped, uncheered, and when the eyes are close and the hands folded, then comes, too late—love enough to have turned the battle and given victory, had it come a little earlier.

Life is hard for many people, and we have no right to withhold any word, or touch or act of love, which will lighten the load or cheer the heart of any fellow-struggler. The best use we can make of our life is to live so that we shall be a blessing to everyone we meet. Then we shall make at least one little spot on this earth more sweet and beautiful, and shall leave a few flowers blooming in the desert when we are gone.

The Summer Vacation

When the vacation season comes, some seekers of rest will settle down in one place for a quiet summer; others flit here and there, from shore to mountain, from mountain to spring, from spring to lake. Some cross the sea and climb the Alps, and hurry through foreign villages and cities. Some go into a secluded spot, away from the distracting noise and noxious smells of the city, and rest where the music of birdsongs breaks continually upon their ears, and the breath of summer flowers sweetens the air about them.

Among these refugees are many thousands of the best Sunday-school workers—pastors, superintendents, teachers, and officers. If they have earned their vacation rest by nine, ten, or eleven months of honest, earnest work—the Master will not blame them for taking it. There is no one who does not need hours and days of pause in his busy life. A few weeks of rest should fit all for better service when they return.

Now, of course, all these Christian workers take their religion with them wherever they go. It is sometimes charged that Christian people leave their religion at home, when they go away for summer vacation or summer travel. But this charge is manifestly untrue. True religion is not like a cloak, something which can be laid off. It is something which begins in the heart and permeates the whole life, weaving its thread into the warp and woof of the character, permeating the disposition, shining in the face, gleaming in the eye, uttering itself in the speech. It is absurd then, to talk about leaving one's religion at home when one travels. All the religion one really has—he will carry with him wherever he goes. People who leave their religion at home, will not have much trouble in laying it off, for it is precious little they can have to leave, and it must be only an outside cloak at the best.

So we may consider this point settled—that all true Christians will take their religion with them. They will be as sincere, faithful, watchful, reverent, prayerful, Bible-reading Christians, by the seashore or on the country farm, as they are at home.

Now let them carry also with them, their Christian activity. After the hard work of nine or ten months some good people think that they should have an absolute rest for the few weeks they spend away from their own fields. So they drop everything. They give up their lesson-study. They keep away from the Sunday-school. They attend church on Sunday mornings—but manifest no interest in the people with whom they worship, or in their work. They make no effort to be helpful to others. They give their hands and hearts a vacation. The result is they leave no impression for good in the place where they have tarried. They fail to let any light shine to cheer or bless other hearts. They fail to bear any positive witness for Christ. They leave no one blessed by their stay.

There is a better way. It is for the Christian worker to continue his active ministry for Christ, wherever he goes. It will not diminish in the smallest degree the benefit he will derive from his vacation. It never aids one's resting or recuperation to be selfish meanwhile. It does one's brain no good to shut up one's heart and stop the outflow of its kindness and beneficence. On the other hand, it makes a vacation all the richer in its results of rest, health, and new vigor—to keep the heart ever open, and to scatter blessings all along one's path.

There are a great many ways in which earnest Christian people can do good in vacation. You are stopping for a few weeks in a country village, or on a farm near a country church. You can enter at once with heartiness and sincerity into the interests of the little congregation. If teachers are needed, you can take a class. If there are young people who are not in the Sunday-school, you may gather a few of them together and form a Bible-class. If no such work seems to be needed, you can enter a class yourself, thus attesting you love for the Bible and your eager desire to know more of it.

At the same time you can make yourself one of the people, showing kindness on every hand, and trying in a simple, Christlike way to touch as many lives as possible with the blessing of your own loving, unselfish spirit. All work for Christ, is not that which we do as officers in church or school. Our *unofficial ministry* is ofttimes far more productive of good results, than that which is formal and official. What we do as Christian men and Christian women, is far more important than what we do as pastors, superintendents, and teachers. There is always a field therefore, and an open door, for the wayside ministry.

Let the spirit of Christ in your heart flow out in gentleness toward all. If you hear of a sick person in the neighborhood, find some way of showing Christian sympathy, by calling, by sending a few flowers, or some choice delicacy, or a little book. If sorrow enters a home while you stay, although you are a stranger, there is nothing improper in your manifesting your interest in some gentle way. You can notice the children whom you meet, win their confidence, and leave blessing in their hearts. If there is a poor family in the vicinity, a widow with orphaned little ones, or a household struggling with adversity—you can prove God's angel to carry help, cheer, and strengthening sympathy.

Or if you are spending the summer in a large boarding-house or hotel. You can gathers the children of the house into a pleasant little Sunday-school which they will greatly enjoy. Or you may arrange for a Bible-reading or a song service on Sunday evenings. There are many Christian ladies and gentlemen who every summer, do such work as this at the boarding-houses or hotels where they spend their vacations; and great good comes from their quiet efforts. In such resorts, too, there is constant opportunity for personal ministry. There are heavy hearts in every such circle as gathers in a large summer boarding-house. There is need for the ministry of sympathy and comfort. There are some who are thoughtless and worldly, who may be impressed, if not by spoken words, at least by the influence of a genuine Christian life, lived out close beside them, in patience, gentleness, and unselfishness, all the summer through.

These are hints only of the ways without number in which true Christian workers may carry on their work through all their summer rest. Wherever they go they will find opportunities, if not for formal, official service, yet always for that better service of heart and tongue and hand to which every Christian is chosen and ordained. They can so witness for Christ in every place—as to win friends for their Master. They can so give out the sweetness of Christian love—that every life which touches theirs shall receive a blessing, and shall bear away an inspiration for better living thereafter. They can so seek to do good to the poor, the sorrowing, the disheartened, that their memory shall be cherished for years in the spots where they tarry.

Is it not better to spend a vacation thus—than in idleness and selfishness, or in worldly gaiety and dissipation?

Launch Out Into the Deep

The deep sea hides great treasures. It is full of wonderful things. It contains a world of beauty. Yet he who only walks along the shore and looks at the shining sands, or picks up here and there a beautiful shell, or watches the waves break on the cold, grey rocks, or he who sails merely along the coast, not venturing out upon the deep waters—knows but little of the wonderful secrets of the sea, which fill its unsunned chambers.

The **BIBLE** is a great ocean. On one shore it breaks on the earth, rolling close to our feet; on the other it dashes up its silver spray on the golden street of heaven. It hides in its depth, the most glorious secrets. The bottom of the sea must hold vast treasures. Ships have gone down with their freightage of gold and silver and precious stones. But in the depths of the Holy Scriptures, are treasures infinitely richer than any which the sea contains. All the wealth of *redemption* is hidden there. There are promises there, and title-deeds to most glorious inheritances, and crowns brighter than any that ever rested on the brow of earthly king, and gem and jewels more brilliant than any that were ever worn in this world. In the depths of Holy Scripture, lie all the riches of God's love and all the treasures of divine knowledge.

But we can never find the wonderful things of the Bible by merely searching along its shores. Newton, after all his discoveries in science, spoke of himself as but a little child playing along the edge of an ocean, finding here and there a brilliant shell, while the ocean itself, with all its great depths, lay before him unexplored. This is still more true of the most diligent researches of the Bible. It is an inexhaustible book. Yet there are those who toil away and draw their nets through it, and find nothing. It is because they search only along the shore. Does the bible yield but little blessing or comfort to us? Do we fail to find in it, the precious things of which we hear others speak? Is it because we have not yet sounded its depths? Its best things come not to mere surface readers; they must be sought for with diligence, with eagerness, with love, with strong faith, with heart-hunger. "Put out into the *depths*, and let down your net," is Christ's word today to us as it was to his disciples.

The same is true of **PRAYER**. It has its great ocean depths. No one has begun to realize the possibilities of prayer. Well says the English poet: "More things are wrought by prayer than this world dreams of." Scientific men are busy measuring the forces of nature. They tell us of the energies of light, of heat, of gravitation, of electricity, and they think they have catalogued all the forces that are at work in this world. But last night a million women were on their knees praying to God for husbands and sons and fathers and brothers, and through the darkness and the silence their pleadings went up to God, and a new power was felt upon a million lives all over the world.

Today, in hundreds of thousands of sanctuaries, devout believers meet and mingle their hearts' breathings in prayers for the outpouring of God's Spirit, and all these importunities are heard in heaven and will bring down upon men's hearts and lives, a spiritual energy that shall be felt in penitences and repentings and new consecrations and obediences, in new holiness and love.

There is something overwhelming in the thought of the things which are wrought by prayer in this world. Think of all the secret prayers which rise from heart-closets, of all the supplications which go up from family altars, of all the pleadings which ascend from worshiping assemblies; and then remember that no true prayer of faith remains unanswered. Truly "more things are wrought by prayer than this world dreams of!"

Yet the great mass of Christian people are only sailing along the shore of the boundless sea of prayer. Take one or two of the promises: "Whatever you shall ask in my name—that will I do." Did Christ mean that? Who will say he did not? "Whatever you shall ask in my name!" Have we sounded that promise to its depths? Have we put it to its full and finest test? Have you brought all your desires to Christ and poured them all out before him? Have we done anything more than walk along the edge of that promise, and picked up a few of the treasures which lie in the shallows?

"Able to do exceeding abundantly above all that we ask or think." What a marvelous ocean of prayer, does this promise unveil to our eyes! Able to do all that we can ask. What can we ask? How much prayer can we put in words? When friends plead for friends; when mothers cry to God for their sick or dying children, or for their children imperiled, unsaved; when pastors supplicate for lost souls perishing in their sins; or when, under sense of need, beseech God for themselves, what desires can they express in words? Then what prayers can we think, which are too great to put into language! We never pray long for anything in deep earnestness, until we find our desires too big for words. We try to tell God of our sorrow for sin, of our weakness and sinfulness; of our desires to be better, to love Christ more; of our hunger after righteousness, after holiness. But with what faltering tongues do we speak! We can put only the merest fraction of our praying into *speech*. But what prayers can we *think*, as we bow before God and breathe out our soul's longings and sighings and hungers and aspirations! "He is able to do exceeding abundantly above all that we ask or *think*." What a measure of the possibility of prayer does this word suggest!

Then have we exhausted the blessing of prayers? Have we sounded its utmost depths? Have we drawn up its richest and best treasures? Do not many of us at times come back from our hours of devotion feeling that nothing has been accomplished? We *ask* and receive but small blessings; we *seek* and find but little gifts; we *knock*, and the door does not seem to open. We *hunger* and get but little bread for our souls. We plead for comfort in our sorrow, and receive only faint gleams of light and mere hints of what we know to be possible. We beseech God to give up his Spirit, and yet how little of the Spirit comes into our life! Is it not true that we have tried only the *shores* of prayer? There are depths into which we have not yet cast our nets. "Launch out into the *deep*, and let down your nets for a catch." We have only to obey his bidding to draw up blessings which shall overwhelm us by their richness and abundance.

Shall we not learn to take God at his word in whatever promises he gives us for prayer? If only we have strong faith, there is no limit to the possibilities of answers to our supplications. Then every pleading will bring down a heavenly benefaction.

Mothers will pray—and their children will be circled around with divine grace. Teachers will pray—and their pupils will come asking how to be Christians. Pastors will pray—and souls will be saved by scores and hundreds, flocking like doves to their windows. Congregations will pray—and the Spirit will come again as on the day of Pentecost, with mighty, resistless power. Mourners will pray—and the sweet comfort of God will come down into their hearts in heavenly blessedness. Christians will pray—and will be filled with all the fullness of God.

God wants to give us infinite blessing. The clouds above us are big with mercy. Let us not hinder the divine blessing, by our prayerlessness, or limit it by our coldness and lack of faith in prayer. Let us launch out into the *deep sea of prayer* and let down our nets, that they may be filled with the best and richest things God has to give.

The same thing is true of **Christian experience**. There are few who really attain to deep and joyous personal experience. There are few who possess a calm and triumphant assurance. The Word of God promises perfect peace to those whose minds are stayed on Christ; but are there are many Christians who realize this deep, tranquil, unbroken peace? Most believers have occasional seasons of joyful, assurance and holy confidence—in the closet, at the communion table, in the house of prayer. Now and then gleams of heavenly sunshine break in upon them and irradiate their souls for a moment—and then the old doubts and fears fill their sky again and shut out the light. The mass of Christian people know but little of abiding spiritual joy—joy which lives on through sorest trials and which nothing can quench. Too much of the joy of Christians, is like *summer flowers* which the first autumn frost kills.

Have we ever thought much of the possibilities of Christian experience? Suppose we take a few Scripture words which describe the privileges of the believer in Christ, and see how much or how little we know by experience of these privileges. "As many as are led by the Spirit of God, there are sons of God. For you received not the spirit of bondage again unto fear; by you received the spirit of adoption, whereby we cry, *Abba, Father!* The Spirit himself bears witness with our spirit, that we are children of God; and if children, then heirs; heirs of God, and joint heirs with Christ."

That is one of Paul's pictures of the believer's privilege. Then here is John's inimitable picture of the same privilege: "Behold what manner of love the Father has bestowed upon us, that we should be called children of God—and such we are!" We know something of what childship means. We have learned it in our own homes. What on earth is more beautiful than childhood in a true, ideal home! How many of us have the child-feeling toward God—perfect love, perfect trust, perfect peace, sweet obedience, filial devotion, and unquestioning acquiescence!

Here is one of Paul's prayers for Christians: "That Christ may dwell in you hearts through faith; to the end that you, being rooted and grounded in love, may be strong to apprehend with all the saints what is the breadth and length and height and depth, and to know the love of Christ, which passes knowledge, that you may be filled unto all the fullness of God." Here again we have hints of what is possible in Christian experience—Christ dwelling in the heart, rooted and grounded in love, strong to know the love of Christ, filled unto all the fullness of God. Have we sounded the depths of such spiritual blessedness as this? Too many of us scarcely ever dare claim to be Christians. We never get beyond "hoping" that we are forgiven and saved. We do not rise to the joy of assurance. We do not exalt and rejoice as God's children, and if children, then heirs. We are not filled with all the fullness of God. We do not know the love of Christ, in the sense that we are conscious ourselves of being loved by Christ with all infinite tenderness.

No doubt many of us have truly blessed experiences in our Christian life. We know something of the love of God, of loving him whom we have not seen, of believing in Christ and clinging to him in the darkness. We know something of communion with God, of fellowship with Christ, of heavenly comfort in sorrow.

This is not questioning the reality of the spiritual life of the humblest believer; it is only saying that most of us have only *tasted* the joy of being Christians. There are far deeper joys within our reach than we have yet experienced. Indeed many of us seem to get very little out of our religion. It does not seem to help us in our struggles with temptation. It does not keep us from being discontented and fretted. It does not light up our sick-rooms. It does not make us victorious in disappointments and sorrow. It does not soften our hearts and make us gentle toward the erring and toward those who injure us. It does not make us brave and heroic in our loyalty to Christ and to the truth. The beauty of the Lord does not shine always in our faces and glow in our characters and appear in our dispositions and tempers. Is this your Christian experience? Is this ordinary Christian life the best that Christ is willing to help us to live? Surely not. We are like the Galilean fisherman—toiling and taking nothing. Is it any wonder some of us are discouraged and are almost ready at times to give up?

But listen to the Master's voice as it breaks upon our ears: "Launch out into the deep, and let down your nets for a catch." The trouble with us, is we have been living in the shallows of God's love. We have been like timid seamen, not venturing out of sight of land, merely dropping our nets along the shore. We have a little faith, a little consciousness of God's love, a little feeling of assurance, a little measure of peace, a little of the child-spirit. But the depths of love, the fullness of joy and peace, the fullness of the blessing of adoption and childship, we have not yet learned. Shall we not strive for richer and more blessed Christian experience? Shall we not push out into the wide sea of God's love? Half consecration knows nothing of the best things of divine grace. We must cut the last chain which binds us back to the shore of this world, and, like Columbus, put out to sea to discover new worlds of blessing.

It is more love we need—more love for Christ. Then more love will give us more faith, and more faith in turn will give us more love. Christian experience begins when we first accept Christ and believe that he loves us, and then commit our lives to him. We begin to trust him, and peace comes as we learn to believe in him and to lay our burdens on him. We know him better and better as we go on trusting him, venturing on him and for him, and following him. So there grows between us and him—a close, tender, intimate fellowship, a friendship more precious than the sweetest of human friendships. The limits of this experience of Christ's love, no one can set. There have been those who have indeed found heaven on earth in their communion with Christ. Let us seek for this today!

What should we do? There is only one thing. We must give ourselves to God as we have never done before. We must open all our soul to the divine Spirit that he may come in and take full possession. We must put away our doubts and fears. We must crucify self—that Christ may be all and in all. We must arouse our spiritual energies until our lives shall be like flames of fire in devotion to God.

The Basis of Helpfulness

There are many people who want to be helpful to others—but who find insuperable obstacles in the way. There are some to whom they find it easy to minister—those of lovely character, those who are their friends and who really reciprocate any favors shown to them. But they must not confine the outgoings of their helpfulness and ministry to such small classes. Even the ungodly do good to those who do good to them, and give to those of whom they hope to receive again. And the Christian must do more. He is to do good to those who hate him, to bless those who curse him, and to be kind to the evil. Even toward unworthy and disagreeable people—he is to manifest that love that is full of gentleness and beneficence.

But how can I help a man whom I cannot respect? How can I be useful to one who treats me with insults or slights? How can I continue to do good to one who only curses me? How can I minister to those who are repulsive in character?

There is a way of relating ourselves to all men, which solves these difficulties. So long as we think of ourselves, and of what is due to us from others, it will be impossible for us to minister to any large number of people. But when true Christian love reigns in the heart, the center of living is removed outside the narrow circle of self. Those who study our Lord's life carefully, will be struck with what we might call *his reverence for humanity*. He looked upon no one with scorn or contempt. The basest fragment of humanity which crept into his presence—trampled, torn, stained, and defiled—was yet sacred in his eyes. He never despised any human being. And further, he stood before men, not as a haughty and imperious king, demanding attention, reverence, honor, service, ministry—but as one who wished to serve, to help, to lift up, to comfort. He said, indeed, that he had not come to be ministered unto—but to minister, and even to give his life for others. He never thought of what was due from men to him, of the attention they ought to show to him, or the honor they ought to accord; but always of what he could do for them, of how he could help or serve them. The more repulsive the life that stood before him—the more deeply, in one sense, did it interest him and appeal to his love, because it needed him and his healing help all the more because of its repulsiveness. And there is no other true basis of helpfulness.

We can learn to do good to all men—only by putting ourselves in the same attitude to them in which our Lord stood to those about him. We must not think of ourselves at all as deserving attention from others, and chafing and fretting if we do not receive it. We are to esteem others better than ourselves, in this sense, especially, that instead of asserting our own superiority and demanding respect, reverence, submission, and service from them—we are in a sense to forget ourselves, and think how we can minister to them. We are not here to be waited upon, honored, and served. The moment we put ourselves in this attitude—we cease to be helpful to others. We then measure everyone by his ability and willingness to serve us. We rate others as they are in our estimation, agreeable or disagreeable. Repulsiveness repels us because we think only of its effect upon our tastes or feelings—and not of what we can do to render it less repulsive. And the result is that we love pleasant people only, are kind to those only who are kind to us, and minister only to the good and gentle. Crude treatment and lack of respect from others—shut our hearts toward them. This may make us very pleasant and agreeable in the small circle of our personal friends, and even in our business and social life, wherever there is room for the play of self-seeking—but it is infinitely removed from the spirit of Christian love and service.

Our Lord drew two pictures, showing the difference between the spirit of the world, and the spirit of Christian life. In the world—men regard greatness as ruling over others, exercising authority, receiving reverence and submission. But in the Christian life—greatness lies in serving. "Whoever will be great among you, let him be your servant." We are to regard ourselves as the servants of others for Jesus' sake. We are to look upon every other person—as one to whom we may render some service.

It will be seen at a glance, that if we look upon others in this purely unselfish way, the whole aspect of the world is changed. We are not here to receive and to gather—but to give and to scatter; not to be served, and exalted, and treated royally—but to serve, regardless of the character of men, or of their treatment of us. This invests every human life with a wondrous sacredness. It brings down our pride, and keeps it under our feet. It changes scorn to compassion. It softens our tones, and divests us of any haughty, imperious, dictatorial manner. Instead of our being repelled by men's moral repulsiveness, our pity is stirred, and our hearts go out in deep earnest longing to heal and to bless. Instead of being offended by men's rudeness and unkindness, we shall find it easy to bear patiently even with ill-treatment, hoping to do them good. We shall continue to seek their good despite their slights, insults, and wrongs. That was the spirit of Christ. Amid human neglect, rejection, persecution, and cruelty—he went right on, thinking only of doing good to others, and never of receiving from them; ministering to the worst, to enemy and friend, with a love which no hate nor malignity could quench, until he poured out his blood upon the cross.

Remembering this, it will no longer be hard for us to do good to the most disagreeable people, to try to help the most unworthy, to be kind to those who are unkind to us, and to spend and be spent for others—even though the more abundantly we love them—the less they love us. It will be easy then to love our enemies, in the only way it is possible for us to love them. We cannot love them as we love our dearest friends. We cannot approve their faults nor commend their immoralities, nor make *black* in them appear *white*. We cannot think their characters beautiful, when they are full of repulsiveness; or their conduct right, when it is manifestly wrong. Love plays no such tricks with our moral perceptions. It does not hoodwink us, nor make us color-blind. It does not make us tolerant of sin, or indifferent to men's blemishes. And yet if fills our hearts with melting tenderness toward all men. In the vilest person, is an immortal soul that Jesus valued so that he did not think his own life too great a price to give for it. And can we be cold toward one in whose life is such worth such possibility of restoration?

Helping by Not Hindering

There are people who only hinder others. Instead of lightening their burdens, they add to them. Instead of being a comfort, they are a constant trial to their friends. Instead of giving cheer, they give disheartenment. They make life harder for others, rather than easier. When such people would heed the counsel, "Bear one another's burdens," the first thing they must learn to do—is to help by not hindering. If they will do this, even though they give no positive help, they will be of much service to those who know them. They will at least cease to be a burden to others, will cease to discourage and dishearten, will cease to impede and tax their friends.

There are a great many hinderers. There are those who are always seeing the dark side. No matter how bright a thing may be, they are sure to find a gloomy view of it. You may paint your hope in most radiant colors—but they will blotch it all with black when they come to look at it. They are always seeing difficulties in the path, lions in the way. They do nothing but prophesy evil, and find out and foretell *difficulties* and *obstacles* in the way of others.

Such people are grievous hinderers. They chill ardor and quench enthusiasm in all those whose lives they touch. Nobody feels quite happy after meeting them; for they manage, even a moment's hurried greeting, to say some *cheerless word* which leaves an unpleasant impression that one cannot shake off. You try to say some pleasant things—but they spoil it by some unfavorable comment. You speak of some bright expectations—but they have a *doubt* ready to darken your clear sky with clouds. You refer to some difficult task before you, which you purpose to accomplish, not thinking of failure; but your *hindering friend* is prompt with suggestions which make you feel that you are not competent to its doing, and when you part from him you have lost your courage and hope, and perhaps you abandon the undertaking which you might otherwise have achieved.

So these people live to make life a little *harder* for all whom they meet. It is impossible to estimate the influence which they exert in retarding, discouraging, and hindering their fellows. This is a miserable and sinful use to make of one's influence to others. Life is hard enough, at best, for everyone; and he who needlessly causes it to be harder for any person—is guilty of wrong to his fellow-man. Instead of making life's load heavier, and the spirit less brave for duty, we should seek to lighten a little of everyone's burden, and to put fresh hope and courage into everyone's heart. We ought at least—to cease to hinder!

We can never know what the final result of a *discouraging influence* may be. When the Israelites were on the edge of the land of promise, ten men came back with a disheartening story of fierce warriors and great giants, and by their cowardly and unbelieving report they started a wild panic of terror among the people. The end of it all was forty years' wandering in a wilderness, and the death there of a whole generation. One discourager may always do immeasurable harm—turning courage to fear, hope to despair, and strength to weakness, joy to sorrow—in many lives. One gloomy prophet, ofttimes retards the progress and hinders the prosperity of a whole community.

These *dishearteners* will do a great service to those who know them—if they will simply cease hindering! Of course, this is only a negative way of helping others; and if the same people would throw all their influence into the other side of the scale, becoming inspirers and strengtheners of others, they would do incalculably more for the good of the world. Yet even this negative *helping by not hindering* would prove a blessing to many lives, although no positive help were thereby given.

Another class of hinderers consists of those who are unnecessarily laying their burdens on others. They have trained themselves into such a condition of dependence, that they can scarcely take a step alone. They want to advise with all their friends, and get a symposium of counsel on everything they do. At the first indication of difficulty or trouble—they fly to someone for help. In cases of real trial, they break down altogether, and have to be carried through on the strong arms of unselfish friends. They are a constant burden to those upon whom they call for sympathy and aid.

Of course, there are cases of real weakness which give one a right to lean on stronger arms, and to be helped and borne along by those who are abler and wiser. No true father or mother ever blames a little child for its helpless dependence, nor regards it as a hinderer of its parents in their life. Nor does anyone with a right heart find fault with those who through disease or misfortune, are unable to toil for themselves or to bear their own burdens, and who must therefore depend on others for support. Nor, again, does anyone grow impatient with the dependence which sorrow or bereavement produces. When one is overwhelmed with grief or crushed by some calamity, there is no Christian man or woman who is not eager to extend sympathy in whatever practical form it may be required. All stand with gentle heart, before human weakness and human need, and are glad to bear the burdens of those who cannot bear their own.

But there are many who are neither little children, nor invalids, nor victims of great sorrow and trial—who yet insist on laying on others the loads which belong to themselves. In this way they also become *hinderers* instead of *helpers*. They think that they believe in the inspired lesson, "Bear one another's burdens, and so fulfill the law of Christ"; but they get only one side of it, availing themselves of its privileges in their need, without ever putting themselves under its requirement on themselves. They believe in others bearing their burdens—but they have no thought of bearing the burdens of others. The other burden-text, "Every man shall bear his own burden," they seem to be wholly ignorant of.

There are loads which none of us have a right to shift to others shoulders, than our own. We have no right to ask others to take their time to attend to our affairs, when we are quite able to attend to our own affairs. We have no right to expect others to solve our little perplexities, and help us bear our little trials, and sympathize with us in our little disappointments, when we are just as strong for these burdens as our friends are. We ought to cultivate self dependence, to think and plan for ourselves, to meet our own questions, to do our own work with our own hands. Especially should we shrink from needlessly becoming a burden to those who love us, or who are patient enough to be willing to help us. We should at least seek to help our friends, by not hindering them unnecessarily with our cares. We should learn the gospel of self-help even if we do not get into our life the other hemisphere of Christian duty—the unselfish side of brotherly help.

And there are many other *hinderers* rather than *helpers* of others. There are those who hinder others by the inconsistencies of their own lives, and by the wrong examples they set. There are those who hinder by their ugly tempers, by their selfishness, by their greed, by their thoughtlessness, by their lack of heart, by their ambition and their pride. There are those who hinder, even when they try to help, by their lack of delicacy and tact. There are many who try to comfort others, who only make worse the hurt which they would heal. If it were possible to eliminate all the needless hindering of others there is in people's lives—this alone would add a large volume to the total of the world's happiness. Then if all the *hinderers* could be made to be *helpers*, a social millennium would have already dawned. Let all of us do our part to usher in that day. At least, let us have a care to help by not hindering.

Bearing One Another's Burden

We hear many an exhortation about the duty of bearing other people's burdens. This is a lesson we should learn. *Living only for one's self, is always sinful.* At certain points in life, and in certain experiences, it is proper also to allow others to share our burdens. We cannot live without brotherly help. It is sad that Napoleon, on the way to Helena, as he noted the fidelity with which everyone on the vessel did his part, remarked that he had never before realized how dependent every man is on others—for the comfort and safety of his life. We are so bound up together, that countless others are continually sharing our burdens and ministering to our needs.

Yet there is a duty of bearing our own burdens which everyone should learn. Many people depend too much on others. They have never trained themselves to answer their own questions, to decide upon their own course in any mater, to attend to their own affairs. They always seek advice and help. By and by, however, in some trying experience, they turn to the old sources of counsel, strength or aid, and find the place empty. Unused to act for themselves, lacking the wisdom, confidence, and ability which training in self-dependence alone can give—they fail, and sink under the burden. If only they had been trained to think and act for themselves, to fight their own battles, to carry their own loads—they would not have been so helpless when caught in the sudden stress of circumstances.

Parents who shelter their children from every rough wind, who think and plan for them, in youth, never accustoming them to burdens, to responsibility, to self care—are not preparing them in the wisest way for life. This is not God's way with us. He does not save us from struggle, from tasks, from thought, from discipline and suffering. He loves us too well for this. He would make us brave, strong, wise, and self-reliant; and therefore he leads us into ways in which we must use every power we have, and develop every slumbering resource in our nature. Thus he prepares us for meeting whatever experiences the future may bring, and trains us for the best character and the largest usefulness.

There are those who have learned to think that others should bear all their burdens for them. They demand service from all about them. They expect everyone to show them attention and favor, to think of their interests and to minister in their advancement. But the quality of character which this spirit fashions, is by no means a beautiful one. It is the very reverse from that which the Master sketched, when he said of himself that "the Son of Man came not to be ministered unto—but to minister." He, the greatest man who ever walked on this earth, exacted nothing from others, claimed no service, and demanded no attention. He lived to serve, to help others, to bear their burdens, to comfort their sorrows.

This is the divine ideal life. If we would realize God's thought of beautiful character, we must not expect others to take care of us, to do our tasks for us—but must quietly and bravely accept the responsibility for our own life, and at the same time use our strength to serve and help others.

There are burdens which we must bear for ourselves, or they never can be borne. There are things which no other one can do for us. If we do not do them, they never will be done. Even God, with his omnipotence, will not do them for us. No other can make our choices, do our duty, meet our responsibility, and answer to God for us. No other can pray to our Father for us, can believe on Christ for us, can get our sins forgiven, can receive divine strength for our weakness.

Ever individual life exists as a separate and distinct entity, filling its own place in the universe, and running its own career. There is something awe-inspiring in the thought of human personality, in its isolation, its individuality, its responsibility, its independence of other personalities while touched by them on all sides. Thousands of other people may be close about us, sharing their life with ours in many ways— and yet in a deep sense each one of us really dwells apart and alone. The heart nearest to ours in love cannot live for us, cannot enter into the inner experiences of our life. Each one must bear his own burden.

This truth is not a mere theoretical one, without practical bearing. It lies at the basis of the only true philosophy of living. No one can make anything of a young man's life but himself. His intellectual powers may be great—but as yet they are only a bundle of possibilities, folded away in his brain, as a stately oak is hidden in the acorn you hold in your hand. These powers must be developed, and this can be done only through a long course of education. In this the young man himself must bear his own burden. He may be sent to the best school—but no school or teacher can bring out the powers that are in his brain, save through his own faithful application and diligent self-disciple. No most affectionate and interested friend can do it. No one can study his lessons for him. No love can relieve him of the burden and toil of the task work, which is necessary in mastering this science of that art.

The price of *education* each one must pay for himself. There is no easy way of attaining it. A rich man can buy many things—but his gold will not purchase for him a trained mind and the treasures of knowledge and culture. He can get these only as the poor man must—by long, patient, unwearying study.

The same is true of *character*. No one can give us the qualities of truth, courage, strength, meekness, gentleness, patience, which belong to the worthy life. We must get them each for himself.

In *experience*, also, it is true that no one can transmit anything to another. We may learn something from what others tell us about the way they have passed over—but the actual lessons each must get for himself. We cannot acquire *sympathy,* from another's suffering. We cannot appropriate the wisdom from another's mistakes and failures, as we can from our own. Every man must bear his own burden.

"Insist upon yourself," exhorts a wise writer. The lesson is important. Most of us depend too little upon ourselves, and lean too much on others. We do not care to bear our own burden. We follow in other's paths, we thresh over and over again other's straw, we gather up the gold which other's have dug out of the rock. Few men are original. It were better for us all if we would insist upon ourselves, if we would let the life that God has given us develop in its own normal way, under the sunshine of divine love. If God has a thought for each life, he will help us to know what this thought is, and then will give us grace to become what he would have us be. While, then, we seek to bear one another's burdens, and cast our own burden upon God, let us each bravely and confidently accept his own burden, and bear it calmly and with faith.

The Ministry of Suffering

Sooner or later, affliction and sorrow come to every Christian. Where is the life, unless it be among the very young, which has experienced no trial? We ought, therefore, to have true views about pain, about the divine reasons for sending it, and about the mission on which it comes. We ought to know, also, how to endure suffering so as to get from it the blessing which its hot hand brings to us.

While they do not solve all the mystery of human suffering, the Scriptures show, at least, that suffering is no accident in God's world--but is one of His messengers; and that it comes not as an enemy--but as a friend on an errand of blessing. The design of God, in all the afflictions which He sends upon His people--is to make them more holy, to advance their purification of character.

It is very clearly taught in the Word of God, that suffering is necessary in preparing sinful souls in this world, for heavenly glory. "We must through much tribulation enter into the kingdom of God." There is no easy way to glory. There is so much evil in us, even after we are born again, that nothing less than the discipline of pain, can cleanse our nature.

Tribulation is God's threshing, not to harm us or to destroy us--but to separate what is heavenly and spiritual in us--from what is earthly and fleshly. Nothing less than blows of pain will do this. The evil so clings to the holy; the golden wheat of godliness is so wrapped up in the strong chaff of the old life--that only the heavy flail of suffering can produce the separation. Perfection of character never can be attained, but through suffering. Holiness cannot be reached without cost. Those who would gain the lofty heights--must climb the cold, rough steeps which lead to them.

It is God's design, in all the pain which He sends--to make us more Christlike. His puts us in the fire of purification, until His own image shines reflected in the gold. His prunings mean greater fruitfulness. In whatever form the suffering comes--the purpose of the pain is merciful. In all our life in this world, God is saving us; and suffering is one of the chief agents which he employs. As Jesus said in one of his Beatitudes, "Blessed are they that mourn—for they shall be comforted." The blessing is not in the mourning—but in the comfort; that is, in the strengthening of the heart to endure the pain victoriously, and get help and better life out of it.

Said Paul: "We also rejoice in our afflictions, because we know that affliction produces endurance, endurance produces proven character, and proven character produces hope." Romans 5:3-4. Suffering works out in us, qualities of Christian character which cannot be developed in any other way. "All chastening seems for the present to be not joyous—but grievous: yet afterward it yields peaceable fruit unto them that have been exercised thereby, even the fruit of righteousness." The present*grievousness of chastening* is forgotten in its "afterward" of ripe fruitage, as winters cold and storm are forgotten in the summer's loveliness and harvest.

But there is a link in the chain, which we must not overlook. Not all afflictions make people better. Tribulation does not always work patience. Chastening does not always, even afterward, yield the peaceable fruit of righteousness. We all have seen people suffering—who became only more impatient, irritable, ill-tempered, and selfish—as they suffered. Many a life *in the furnace of affliction* loses all the beauty it ever had. It is not by any means universally true, that we are made more holy and Christlike, by pain. There are dangerous shoals skirting the deeps of affliction, and many frail barques are wrecked in the darkness. In no experience of life do most people need wise friendship and firm, loving guidance more than in their times of trouble.

This subject is of such vital importance that we should give it our most earnest thought, not dismissing it from our minds until we have learned how trial must be endured so as to get blessing from it. For one thing, we must make sure of our personal relation to Christ. Two bare trees stood side by side one early spring. The sun poured down its warm beams and soon one of them was crowned with bursting buds, and later with rich foliage; but the other was still bare. One tree had life, and the other was dead. Where there was life, the hot sun called out beauty; where life was wanting, the effect of the heat was to make the tree appear even more completely dead. Affliction comes to two lives side by side; one life becomes more Christ-like, while the other withers in the heat. In the one, there is spiritual life; in the other, there is no life. There must be personal faith in Christ—or pain will not leave blessing.

Then again, the affliction must be received as God's messenger. We imagine that all angels wear radiant dress, and come to men with smiling face and gentle voice. Thus artists paint them. But truly they come ofttimes in very somber garb, and it is only when we receive them in faith, that they disclose to us their merciful aspect and mission.

We should therefore receive afflictions reverently, as sent from God. Even in our tears we should accept its message as divine. We may be assured that there is always some blessing for us, in pain's hot hand. There is some golden fruit, wrapped up in the rough husk. God designs to burn off some sins from us, in every fire through which he calls us to pass. Not to be able to accept from our Father's hand, the seed of pain, is to miss the fruits of blessing which can grow from no other sowing. We should give sorrow, when it comes, just as patient, loving welcome as we give joy; for it is from the same hand, and has the same errand to us. It is when we receive pain in this spirit that it blesses us. *No one who murmurs under God's chastening hand, is ever made better by it.*

Then, to get the benefit of the ministry of suffering, we must find true comfort. Many people suppose that if they can dry their tears, and resume again their old familiar course of life, they have been comforted. They think only of getting through the trial, and not of getting anything of *help* or *blessing* out of it. The true aim of suffering is to get from it--more purity of soul, and greater revelations of God's face, more of the love of Christ in the heart, and fresh strength for obedience and all duty. An old Psalm writer said: "Before I was afflicted I went astray; but now have I kept your word." That is true comfort—holier, better living.

Out of every experience of pain, we ought to get something good. When we have passed through a season of suffering, and stand beyond it, there ought to be a new light in our eye, a new gentleness in our touch, a new sweetness in our voice, and a new hope in our heart. We ought not to permit our grief to flow long in bitter tears—but should turn it quickly into channels of earnest devotion and active usefulness. True comfort puts deep joy into the heart, and anoints the sufferer with a new baptism of grace and power.

One Christian woman wrote to another woman in deep grief: "The shadow of death will not always rest on your home; you will emerge from its obscurity into such light as they who have not sorrowed cannot know." This was true even of the earthly experience after sanctified sorrow; but it is true in a far deeper sense of the heavenly "afterward" of pain accepted as God's messenger. Not only will the sorrow of death be forgotten in the joy of heaven—but the joy of heaven will be far deeper and richer because of earth's pain and sorrow.

Your Will Be Done

The whole liturgy of *absolute consecration* is written out in full in this one brief petition. It is a prayer that we may be made perfect and complete in all the will of God. This is the standard of living which our Lord lays down in almost every chapter of his gospel. There can be no lower condition of discipleship deduced from any of his teachings.

On a summer's evening, a boy stood in thoughtful mood intently gazing up into the calm, silent depths of the skies. His face wore an anxious, troubled look. His mother, drawing near, asked him what he was thinking of. "I was thinking," he replied, "how far off heaven is, and how hard it must be to get there." She was a wise mother, and out of the experience of her own heart she said, "Heaven must first come to you, my boy; heaven must first come into your heart." Never was truer word spoken. That was what Jesus meant when he said, "Except a man be born again—he cannot see, or enter into, the kingdom of heaven." That was what he meant when he said again, "The kingdom of God is *within* you."

What makes heaven? Not its jeweled walls, and pearly gates, and streets of golden pavement, and crystal river, and burning splendor—but its blessed obedience, its sweet holiness, its universal and unbroken accord with the divine will. Heaven, as a home, can never be entered by anyone in whose heart the spirit of heaven is not found. We are fitted for the blessedness of that *home of glory* just in the measure in which we have learned to do God's will on the earth—as it is done in heaven.

Then, sometimes, the form of the obedience is *passive*. God's ways are not as our ways. His plans frequently move right through our plans in their stately marches. Ofttimes the petition of, *"May your will be done"* must be offered, if offered at all, when it means the relinquishment of the dearest treasures and fondest hopes of our hearts, or the patient, joyful endurance of the keenest sufferings and the sharpest self-denials. We are not only to do the will of God in our busy activities—but to allow it to be done *in* us and respecting us, even when it crushes us to the very earth!

Do we quite understand this? It seems to me that it is something far more profound than many of us think. It is not *mere acquiescence*. This may be stoical and obstinate, or it may be despairing and hopeless. Neither temper is the true one. Nothing less is involved in the prayer, than the *utter and absolute consecration of our lives and wills—to the will of God.*

A right understanding of this petition, is about the doctrine of prayer and its answer. We pray, and the answer does not come. In our bitter disappointment we say, "Has not God promised that if we ask—we shall receive?" Yes—but Jesus himself prayed that the *cup of his agony*—the betrayal, the trial, the ignominy, the crucifixion, and all that nameless and mysterious woe which lay behind these apparent things— might pass, and it did not pass. Paul prayed that his thorn in the flesh might be removed. All along the centuries mothers have been agonizing in prayer over their dying babes, crying to God that they might live; and even while they were praying, the shadow deepened over them, and the little hearts fluttered into the stillness of death. All through the Christian years, crushed hearts under heavy crosses of sorrow and shame, have been crying, "How long, O Lord, how long?" and the only answer has been a little more *suffering* added to the burden, another *thorn* in the crown of shame.

Are not prayers answered, then, at all? Certainly they are. Not a word that goes faith-winged up to God, fails to receive attention and answer. But ofttimes the answer that comes is not relief—but the spirit of acquiescence in God's will. The prayer, many, many times, only draws the trembling suppliant closer to God. The cup did not pass; but the will of Jesus was brought into such perfect accord with his Father's, that his piteous cries for relief died away in words of sweet, peaceful yielding. The thorn was not removed—but *Paul* was enabled to keep it and forget it in glad acquiescence in his Master's wish. The child did not recover— but *David* was helped to rise, and wash away his tears, and worship God.

Do not think that every burden you ask God to remove—he will remove; or that every favor you ask him to bestow—he will bestow. He has never promised to do so. Moreover, the first wish in your praying is not to be to get the blessing or the relief you desire. This would be putting your own will before God's. It would be striking out this petition from the Lord's lesson in your praying. The first, the supreme wish should ever be that God's will, whatever it may be, may be done. We are to say, "This desire is very dear to me; I would like to have it granted; yet I cannot choose, and I put it into your hand. If it be your will, grant me my request. If not, withhold it from me, and help me sweetly and joyfully to acquiesce."

Your health is broken. It is right to pray for its restoration; but running all through your most earnest supplication, should be the songful, trustful, peaceful, "Nevertheless, not my will—but yours, be done." You are a mother, and are struggling in prayer over a sick child. God will never blame you for the strength of your maternal affection, or for the clasping, clinging which that holds your darling in your bosom, and pleads that it be not taken from you. Love is right; mother-love is right, and of all things on earth is most like the mighty love of God's own heart. Prayer is right, no matter how intense or how earnest. It is right that you should want to keep that beautiful life. Yet, amid all your agony of desire, this should still be the supreme, the ruling wish, controlling all, subduing and softening all of nature's wild anguish—that God's will may be done. In all your strong supplications, the refrain of Gethsemane must be heard—"Not as I will—but as you will."

The first thing always, before any unburdening of our own heart's load, before any laying down of crosses or averting of trials or sorrows, before any gratification of our own desires—is to be that God's will may be done. We are to have desires—but they are to be subordinate to God's desire, which must be far wiser and better than ours. We are to make plans—but they are to be laid at God's feet, that he may either take them up into his own plan as parts thereof, or set them aside and give us better plans. Utter consecration, joyous, loving, intelligent, willing consecration to the will of God, is the standard of Christian living, which this petition sets up before us.

The Cost of Carelessness

How often do we hear as an excuse for some harm done or committed, *"I did not mean to do it. I had no thought of causing any such trouble."* Certainly "lack of thought" draws after it a great train of evils, and leaves behind it a broad trail of cost and sorrow. We see the results of *carelessness* in all departments of life, and in all degrees, from the most trivial, causing only inconvenience and confusion, to the most far reaching, casting a shadow into eternity.

A nurse fell down the stairs with an infant in her arms, and fifty years afterward there was a humpbacked man creeping along the streets. A child threw a piece of lemon peel on the sidewalk, and there was an accident an hour after, in which an old lady was severely injured; so severely that she will never be able to walk again. A switch-tender opened the wrong switch, and the heavy train dashed into a great building that stood at the end of the short side-track, and lives were lost amid the wreck. An operator gave a careless touch to his instrument, and there was a terrible collision on the rail. A boy shot an arrow from his bow; it went whizzing away from the string, and a comrade is blind for the rest of his life. A woman poured oil from a can into her stove to hasten her fire, and there was an explosion, and an outburst of flame, which burned down the building around her. A young man pointed a gun, in sport, at his best friend, playfully saying that he would shoot him, and one noble youth was carried to his grave, and another goes through life with an awful shadow of memory hanging over him, which quenches all his joy and makes all life dark for him. A druggist's clerk compounded the prescription in haste, and in an hour a sick girl was dying in terrible pain and convulsions, from the poison in the prescription.

A beautiful young lady danced at a party one chill midnight, and then raised a window in a side room to let the fresh air fan her hot cheeks; and in a little while they followed her to an untimely grave. What long chapters of accidents are every year recorded, all of which result from carelessness! A little careful thought on the part of the responsible people would have prevented all of them, with their attendant horrors and their long train of suffering and sorrow.

There are other illustrations. Millions of *letters* every year go wrong, fail to reach their destination, and find their way to the dead-letter office, because the writers carelessly misdirect them. A gentleman lost an overcoat. His suspicions fell on a neighbor, and a trap was laid to detect his guilt; but after a great deal of wicked feeling—the coat was found precisely where the owner had left it. Many a servant is abused and wronged and cruelly treated, on charges with similar ground. A Boston man coming home in a drenching rain, felt for his watch at his doorstep, to see the time; but it was missing. He had been robbed. He remembered it all—just a few doors back a man rubbed against him in passing. He was the thief. He flew after him, overtook him, raised his umbrella and demanded his watch, or he would strike. The terrified man handed it to him, and the good citizen went home, proud of his courage and success. The morning paper told of a bold highway robbery, a most daring affair. The robber lifted an enormous club, and was about to kill the quiet pedestrian. It happened just close by this gentleman's house. "That is strange," he said, as his wife read the account at breakfast; "I was robbed of my watch, and overtook the thief at that very spot, and recovered it." His wife assured him there must be some mistake, as he had left his watch at home the morning before, and she had since noticed a strange one on the bureau. So it turned out that he was the robber.

There is a great deal of the same lack of carefulness in other ways, whose consequences are not so manifest, and yet are no less painful and destructive. A man speaks light and careless words, perhaps in humorous mood, perhaps in impatience and irritation, and while the laughter goes around—a heart is writhing in agony, pierced by the cruel barb. He did not mean to give pain to that tender friend; he would not do it intentionally for the world; but he has left a wound and a pang there, which no after kindness can altogether heal and soothe. There is a manifold ministry of pain and wrong, wrought thus by carelessly uttered words. Some people appear always to say the very things they ought not to say. Hawthorne says that *awkwardness* is a sin which has no forgiveness in heaven or on earth. And surely *carelessness* is laden with the guilt of countless griefs and sorrows, which no after-penitence can ever remove, or even palliate and soften.

A person's name is mentioned in a certain circle, or in a quiet conversation, and the most inexcusable liberties taken in speaking of him, his character, his business, and his acts. No one means to do him harm or injustice; and yet, in the guise of confidence, words are uttered which are like so many cruel stabs.

Few habits are more common than this; and yet what rights have we to say one defamatory word of another, or start, even by a hint, a suspicion of him? We may plead that we have no intention of injuring him—but the pleas avails nothing. We are responsible not only for our deliberate, purposed acts—but just as much so for the accidental and unconscious effects which go out from us. They say that every word spoken into the air goes quivering on, in undying reverberations, forever. Whatever we may say of this statement as a scientific fact—we are well aware of the infinite and far-reaching consequences of the smallest words as moral forces. The poet's fancy is not a mere play of imagination. The *song* we sing, and the *word* we speak—we shall indeed find again, from beginning to end, somewhere in the eternal future, stored away in the nooks and crannies of other lives, and influencing them for good or ill, for pain or pleasure.

There is no part of this life we are living, day by day, that is not vital with influence. We call certain things *small* and *infinitesimal*, and indeed they seem so; but when we remember that there is not one of them that may not set in motion a train of eternal consequences, dare we call anything insignificant? We are evermore touching other lives, oftener unconsciously than consciously, and our touch today may decide a destiny. Our *silent example*, as well as our *words* and *deeds*, is vital, and throbbing with influence. There is need, therefore, for the most unwearying watchfulness over every act and word, lest in a moment of unheeding, we start a train of consequences that may leave sorrow or ruin in its track forever.

Nowhere is this more important than in dealing with souls, as spiritual teachers and guides. Milton somewhere says, that bad advice may slay not only a life—but an immortality. Bad or careless religious counsel may wreck a soul's destiny. Should a teacher ever sit down before a class of immortal souls, looking up with confidence for guidance, without the most diligent and thoughtful preparation as to what to say to them? Carelessness anywhere else may be pardoned, sooner than here.

Jesus Consecrating All Life

In his passage through life, in all its phases of growth and development, Jesus sanctified all pure relationships and experiences. He sanctified *childhood*. Childhood has been sanctified, its joys sweetened, and its sacredness enhanced, by the human infancy of Jesus.

So he sanctified *motherhood*, since of a human mother, was born the incarnate God; since on a human mother's bosom he lay, clasping his tiny arms about her neck.

So he sanctified *home*. Whatever is truly sacred, pure, tender, and holy in our homes, comes from his life in this world. What a home that Nazareth home must have been! Think of that lovely, sinless, joyous life growing up there, through tender infancy—bright beautiful youth, noble, spotless manhood. One patient, gentle spirit in any home is enough to fill all the household life with unspeakable sweetness and peace. But think of Jesus, his wondrous beauty, his benignity, his self-forgetfulness, his prayerful piety, his divine purity, his joyous affectionateness, his unruffled calm. And ever since, Christianity has been a home religion. It purifies home joys, softens home sorrows, and sanctifies home relationships.

So Jesus blessed *poverty*, for he lived as a poor man. He blessed toil; for his own hands grew hard as he wrought. He blessed *social life*, for he grew in favor with his fellow-men; no stern ascetic—but mingling in the circles of his friends, and pouring the fragrance of his gracious character on all about him.

Then at length he went away from the privacy and quiet of the home, and for three years longer, touched life at all its higher and lower points. He met *temptation's* stern assaults, being tempted at all points like as we are. He learned very soon what it was to be *hated*: what it was to *love* intensely—and not to be loved in return; what it was to receive only scorn—for all his pitying compassion; what it was to want to bless and help others—and to have them turn away and refuse his gifts and help; what it was to be grieved and disappointed, and have men draw away from his influence, and slip down to ruin. He learned what it was to be rejected, even by his family. He knew what it was to be homeless and friendless, with an atmosphere of icy hate all about him. He knew what it was to be *betrayed* by one he had cherished for years as a friend, to be *denied* by another, to be *forsaken* by all, and to stand utterly alone in the center of the world's rage and cruelty.

I have merely touched upon these points in his human experience, to show that he has sanctified all life. He touched humanity at every point, from the tenderness and innocence of the new-born babe, to the lowest depth of sorrow and shame.

All of life is holy now. We all know how human love consecrates for us whatever it touches. You treasure a little picture; you keep it in your own room; gold would not buy it. It is neither beautiful nor valuable as a work of art; yet there is nothing in the galleries that has for your eye, such loveliness. It was your mother's; her hands made it. How sacred is a book whose pages a loving friend used to turn and read. How we prize anything that love has touched! How sacred are the paths affection's feet have pressed—the room, the chair, the pen, the table, the cup, the ring, made precious by love's memories! *All of life is rendered sacred by the touch, the footprint, the heart-thrill of Jesus.*

It ought not to be so hard for us to live when we remember this. Whatever the experience, we know that Jesus once felt the same that we feel. This is nothing strange to him. He understands; he sympathizes; he knows who to help.

How to Get Help From Church Services

How to get from public church services the help they have to give to us—is one of the most important practical questions to which attention can be turned. Private devotion is not enough; the honor of God and the needs of our spiritual nature alike, require associated worship. To neglect the public services, is to deprive ourselves of one of the greatest aids to religious culture. No doubt there are rich possibilities of spiritual help in these services, if we know how to find it. The question is worth considering.

It is quite possible to attend church services, even with commendable regularity, and yet receive no spiritual profit. There is no holy atmosphere in the house of God—which is in itself medicinal or healthful to our souls. There is no filtration of grace into our hearts, which goes on unconsciously and without agency of our own, while we sit in our soft pew in the sanctuary. Forms of worship, whether plain or elaborate, are empty—without the sincere homage and faith of loving hearts. They carry up to God—just what we put into them; they bring down to us from God—just what we, with prayer and faith, draw out of them. Two people may sit side by side, and take like part in the exercises of devotion; yet from one rises to God pure incense and an acceptable offering; and from the other the empty mockery of a heartless and formal service. The one goes away strengthened and blessed, and the other carries away but a cold, unblessed heart. Whatever the forms of public worship may be, the heart must be engaged, or the worship is vain and unprofitable.

To make this chapter as helpful as possible, a few definite suggestions are offered.

To begin with, *thoughtful preparation* for the church services will greatly increase their profitableness to those who engage in them. The very best ordinary preparation is a season of private devotion, before going to the sanctuary. The heart is thus cleansed of its worldly thoughts, is opened and warmed toward God, and is in a suitable condition to enter sincerely and earnestly into the public worship.

A *reverent* approach toward, and entrance into, God's house is a further aid to blessing in the services. We should at least know and consider well—on what errand we are going to meet God—to worship him and receive help for our own lives—and should have our expectations aroused in anticipation of the communion with God and his people which we are so soon to enjoy, and our hearts eager with desire for the holy meeting. Our age is not reverent. Many people enter God's house with as little seriousness as if it were a concert or a literary entertainment, which they had come to hear. Such people are not prepared either to render acceptable worship, or to receive needed help. We shall find in God's house, just what we come spiritually prepared to find. God must be in the heart—or we shall not see God in the exercises of worship. We shall never find in the sanctuary, that which we do not really seek and earnestly want to find. If we enter careless and indifferent, with no spirit of devotion—we shall carry away no blessing. If we come with longing and earnest desire to meet God, and lay our burdens at his feet, to rest and refresh ourselves in his presence, and to receive new strength from him for duty—we shall find all that we wish.

Another condition of help, is earnest personal interest in each part of the service. There is no blessing in our being merely among true worshipers, and in the presence of God. A throng was close around Christ one day—but only one of them was healed; and she was healed because she reached out her trembling finger, and in faith touched the hem of Christ's garment. This history may be repeated any Sunday in any congregation. While the multitude throngs close about Christ, those alone who touch the hem of his robe—will receive blessing. Even in public services, we do not worship in companies—but as individuals. One sitting close beside us may hold delightful communion with God, and receive rich spiritual refreshment, while our heart remains like a dry, parched field, receiving not one drop of rain from the full overhanging clouds.

Then after the service, we should go away as thoughtfully and reverently as we came. The custom prevalent in some churches, of lingering a moment in silent prayer after the blessing is very beautiful and impressive. Church-aisle sociability, so often commended, no doubt has its pleasant side; but it certainly has its disadvantages and its grave dangers. We may greet each other cordially and affectionately in quite tones as we pass out, without spiritual harm; but too often the conversation runs either into criticism of the preacher or the sermon, or off on trivial and worldly themes. In either case the good seed sown—is picked up by the birds and devoured before it has had time to root! We had better go away quietly, pondering the great thoughts which the service has suggested to us, seeking to deepen in our hearts, the impressions made—and to assimilate in our lives, the truths of God's Word which have fallen upon our ears.

From the church gate back again to the closet whence we set out—is the best walk to take after the service has closed. A few moments of secret prayer will carry the blessings of the sanctuary so deep into our hearts that they will be thereafter part of our very life.

Then, in the busy week-days which follow, come the proofs of the helpful influences and blessings which have flowed into our lives in the Sunday services. The food which is eaten today—is the strength of the laborer, the eloquence of the orator, the skill of the artisan, tomorrow. The spring sunshine and rain which fall upon the dry briery rose bush, reappear in due time in fragrant lovely roses. So sincere and true worship, in the quiet Sunday hours, will show itself in the beautiful character, the sweeter spirit, the brighter hope, the truer better living, and the holier consecration—of the days of toil and struggle which make up the week.

The Value of Devotional Reading

All reading ought to be a means of grace. We should never read any book which will not leave in mind and heart some helpful, strengthening, or uplifting thought. This is not saying that we should never read any but *distinctly Christian* books. All truth is enriching. History, if rightly read, inspires adoring feeling. Books of *science* help us to think over again God's thoughts, and thus stimulate reverence. *Poetry*, if true and pure, is wondrously elevating, even though it may not treat of spiritual themes. Good *fiction* may teach us noble lessons in conduct, sketch for us the loftiest things in character, and inspire in us, "whatever things are true, whatever things are lovely." Even *humor* has its place as a means of grace. There are times when what a good man needs above all things—is a hearty laugh. The man who writes truly witty things, has a mission. Thus there is no good book of any order, which may not have its place in helping us to grow in grace.

Yet there is a special class of books which may fitly be used as *devotional helps*. When we speak of devotions, we usually refer to the "silent times" which every earnest Christian must get into his days, even the busiest of his days. Much is said of the necessity of secret prayer. Perhaps not enough is said of the necessity of *devotional reading* as part of the exercise of devotion. It is not enough to speak to God to tell him of our needs, our dangers, our sins, our troubles; and to plead with him for help, for favor, for comfort. We must also let God talk to us. We must feed our souls. No pious exercise is complete, without the reading of some sentence or sentences which will start in the mind uplifting thoughts, give us a suggestion of a new lesson to be learned, show us a glimpse of spiritual beauty to be reached after, or speak to us a word that we may rest on in our weakness, or take as rod and staff in the valley.

Of course the Bible is always to be the first book in such exercise. It is never to be left out. A "silent time" with prayer, and yet without a verse or more of the simple Word of God, lacks an essential element. We must hear God speak to us—while we speak to him. Perhaps the best of all devotional exercises is illustrated in the oft-told incident of *Bengel*. He was known to be much in prayer, to spend long seasons of time in his private devotions. Someone was curious to know something of the way he prayed, and hid himself in the good man's study one evening to watch him at his secret devotions. Bengel sat long at his table with his New Testament open before him. He read on quietly, yet uttered no word of prayer that the watcher could hear. Sometimes he would pause over a verse, and his face would glow and his eyes would be turned upward—but he did not speak. At length the clock struck midnight, and then the saintly man clasped his hands on the open book, and said, "Dear Lord Jesus, we are on the same old terms." That was all the curious intruder heard. Yet for an hour or longer the loving heart had been holding sweet converse with Christ.

Such an hour is worth a thousand of the hurried, stereotyped "secret prayers" which many Christians make, ofttimes without any true devotion or real communing. When we sit down with our best friend, we do not merely ask a few favors, and make a few complaints, and utter a few groans, and then run away. We commune with our friend. We may ask no favor at all; rather we seek to have our hearts flow together in love, as we converse on themes that are sacred to us both. Secret prayer should not be merely an unburdening of our heart, a telling of our needs and desires to God. It should be far more than this. We should get quiet, that God may speak to us, that his love may flow into our heart, that his life may enter our soul.

The Bible is the first book of devotion, essential, indispensable, never to be left out of the closet library, never to be unused in even the briefest time with God. But there are many other books which may be used with great profit besides and with the Bible. There are some men who have a peculiar gift for the interpreting of the Bible. They find the beautiful things in it, which many others do not seem to be able to find. They have facility in showing us the deeper meanings of the Scripture words. They elucidate the teachings of inspiration, in such a way as to make our hearts burn within us, as we read what they have written. Books of such writers are peculiarly helpful in the closet. If we read a chapter from one of them, or a few pages, or possibly one a paragraph or two, we shall have some scriptural truth shining with new beauty in our heart when we leave our closet, or we shall have a fresh impulse toward some important duty, or we shall have a vision of spiritual loveliness glowing before us which shall draw us toward more heavenly living; or, if we are in sorrow, we shall carry away some precious comfort which shall give us sweet peace.

Such *devotional interpretation of the Scriptures* is always helpful in the closet. It is strange how precious Bible truths will elude the eye of a reader, sometimes for years, though he read the chapters over and over again. Then one day, a few sentences in a sermon or in a book will lift them out of their hiding place, and they will flash in brilliant beauty. What we need in the way of interpretation for such reading of the Bible as will bless our lives—is the *application* of its great teachings to common, daily, practical life. A paragraph which takes a Scripture text, and so opens it for us in the morning that all day long it helps us to live, becoming a true lamp to our feet, and a staff to lean upon when the way is rough—is the very best devotional help we can possibly have. Most people need to have the Bible explained to them—at least, they find great benefit in such real opening of its words.

Take an example. You read a few sentences which explain to you the meaning of the words: "Cast your burden upon the Lord—and he shall sustain you." You are reminded that, in the margin of your reference Bible, "gift" is suggested as another reading for "burden." Then you are reminded further that in the Revised Version the marginal reading suggest a further amplification of the word, so that the phrase reads: "Cast what he has given you upon the Lord." So your burden, whatever it is, is something which God has given you—a gift of God to you. Hence it is sacred, and carries folded up in it a blessing. This opening of the Scripture changes the whole aspect of your burden.

You are reminded further—that there is no promise here that this burden will be taken away, the assurance is that you will be *sustained* in bearing it. This *gift* of God is a *blessing*, and you cannot afford to have it taken away from you. You must keep it—but you will be enabled to bear it. One who finds such an opening of the text as this in his morning reading, has acquired food for a whole day, which will prove also an interpretation for life. Every chapter in the Bible is meant to help us to live, and there can be no better reading for private devotion than that which really opens the Scriptures for us.

Another class of devotional reading of great practical value is poetry. Some people always sing hymns as part of their private worship. If this is not practicable, the reading of good, uplifting hymns has great value as a means of spiritual culture. It warms the heart and kindles praise and adoration.

The chief thought to be emphasized here, is that we need to *read* as well as to *pray*; otherwise we shall not grow. The Bible is always the first book to be used. But most people need help in the interpretation of the Bible—so as to get from it the precious things which are folded up in its words. Hence there is always a place for books of the right kind, on the closet table.

The Value of Communion With God

Some of the saddest cries that wail out in the Psalms, are sighings for the joy of the divine presence, temporarily lost. And when we come to think of it, there is no other loss in all the range of possible losses, which is as great as the breaking of our communion with God. This is not the ordinary estimate. We speak with heavy heart—of our earthly sorrows. When bereavements come, and our homes are emptied and our tender joys borne away—we think there is not grief like ours. Our lives are darkened, and very dreary does this earth appear to us as we walk its paths in deep loneliness. Then there are other losses—losses of friends by alienation; losses of property, of comforts, of health, of reputation.

But there is not one of all these, which is such a calamity—as the loss of God's smile, the hiding of his face, or the interruption of our fellowship with him. Men sigh over their misfortunes which touch only their earthly circumstances, and forget that there is no misfortune like the *decay of spirituality* in their hearts. It would be well if all of us understood this. There are earthly misfortunes under which hearts remain all the while warm and tender, like the flower-roots beneath the winter's snows, ready to burst into glorious bloom when the springtime comes. And there are worldly prosperities under which spiritual life withers and dies.

We do not know what God is to us—until, in some way, we lose the sense of his presence and the consciousness of his love. This is true of all our blessings. We do not know their value to us—until they are lost or imperiled. We do not prize *health* until it is shattered and broken, and we can never have it restored again. We do not recognize the richness and splendor of *youth* until it has fled, with all its glorious opportunities, and worlds cannot buy it back. We do not appreciate the comforts and blessings of *Providence* until we have been deprived of them, and are driven out of warm homes into the cold paths of a dreary world. We do not estimate the value of our facilities for education and improvement, until the period of these opportunities is gone, and we must enter the hard battle of life unfurnished and unequipped. We do not know how much our *friends* are to us—until they lie before us silent and cold. Ofttimes the vacant chair, or the deep, unbroken loneliness about us—is the first revealer of the worth of one we have never duly prized.

In like manner, we do not know the blessedness of fellowship with God until his face is darkened, or he seems to have withdrawn himself. Jesus never seemed so precious to the disciples—as when they had him no more. Two of his friends, indeed, never made an open confession of their love for him at all, until his body hung upon the cross. They had loved him secretly all along; but now, as they saw that he was dead, and they could never, as they supposed, do anything more for him, or enjoy his presence again—all their heart's love awoke in them, and they came boldly out and asked for his body, took it down tenderly in the sight of the multitude, and bore it away to loving burial. But for his death—they would never have known how much they loved him, nor how much he was to them!

And I am sure that David never knew what God and God's house were to his soul—until he was driven away from his home and city and could no more enter the sanctuary. As he fled away, it seemed as if his heart would break, and his deepest sorrow was not for the joys of home left behind, for throne and crown and palace and honors—but for the house of God, with its hallowed and blessed communion. All the other bitter griefs and sorrows of the hour were forgotten, or swallowed up, in this greatest of all his griefs—separation from God's presence. I do not believe that the privileges of divine fellowship were ever so precious to him before, while he enjoyed them without hindrance, as when he looked from his exile towards the holy place and could not return to it.

And does not the very *commonness* of our spiritual blessings conceal from us, their inestimable value to us? Luther somewhere says, "If in his gifts and benefits God were more sparing and close-handed, we would learn to be thankful." The very unbroken continuity of his favors—causes us to lose sight of the Giver, and to forget to prize the gifts themselves. If there were gaps somewhere, we would learn to appreciate the wealth of the divine goodness to us. Who is there among us all, who values highly enough—the *tender summer of God's love* which broods over us with infinite warmth evermore?

Do we value our privileges as Christians, and improve them—as we would if for a season, we would be deprived of them? Our church privileges, our open Bibles, our religious liberty, our Sunday teaching and communings, our hours of prayer—do we prize these blessings as we would—if we were suddenly torn away, by some cruel fortune, and cast in a land where all these are lacking? Do we appreciate our privileges of fellowship with God as we would—if his love would be withdrawn, and the light of his presence put out?

There is something very sad in the thought that we not only fail to value the rich blessings of God's love—but that we oftentimes thrust them from us, and refuse to take them, thereby wounding the divine heart and impoverishing our own souls. It would be very bitter if any of us should first be made really aware of the presence and grace of Christ—by his vanishing forever from our sight, after having stood at our locked and bolted doors, in wondrous patience, for long years. It would be a bitter thing to learn the glorious blessedness of the things of God's mercy and love—only by seeing them *depart* forever beyond our reach.

There is another phase of this subject, which ought to bring much comfort to those who are called to suffer earthly losses. If we have *God* left to us—no other loss is irreparable! A gentleman came home one evening with a heavy heart, and said that he had lost everything he had. Bankruptcy had overtaken him. "We are utterly beggared!" he said. "All is gone—there is nothing left!" His little girl of five years, crept up on his knee, and, looking earnestly into his despairing face, said, "Why, papa, you have mamma and me left." Yes, what is the loss of money, stores, houses, costly furniture, musical instruments and works of art—while love remains?

There is surely enough in God's love, to compensate a thousand times for every earthly deprivation! Our lives may be stripped bare—home, friends, riches, comforts, every sweet voice of love, every note of joy—and we may be driven out from brightness and music and tenderness and shelter into the cold ways of sorrow; and yet if we have God himself left—ought it not to suffice? Are not all earth's blessings gifts from God to us? And is he not able to give us again all that we have lost? Yes, is he not *himself* infinitely more than all his gifts? If we have him, have we not all things in him?

Therefore it is, that so often we do not learn the depth and riches of God's love, and the sweetness of his presence—until other joys vanish out of our hands, and other loved presences fade away out of sight. The loss of temporal things empties our hearts—to receive unseen and eternal things. The sweeping away of earthly hopes reveals the glory of our heart's refuge in God. Someone has beautifully said, "Our refuges are like the nests of birds; in summer they are hidden among the green leaves—but in winter they are seen among the naked branches." Worldly losses but strip off the foliage, and show us our heart's warm nest in the bosom of God!

The Birthday of the New World

The world is growing old. We date time from the birth of Jesus Christ, as if there had been no years before he was born. The truth is, there were many long centuries before that time—no one knows how many. But somehow *centuries without Christ* do not count for much. The years seem like long rows of ciphers, with no numeral preceding them to give them value. At least, from the day Christ was born into this world—all things had a new meaning.

Perhaps we do not think often of the real significance of the abbreviations A.D., which we use continually in noting time. They tell us that the years in which we are living and all the years that have passed since Jesus was born are years of our Lord.

They are years of his stay in this world. The birth of Jesus was indeed a new beginning of time. From that day forward there was something in this world that never had been in it before. It was not merely new teaching, although "no man ever spoke like this man." The words of Jesus have been seeds of blessing, all these nineteen centuries. It was not merely the life of a great man, like other men whose names have immortal honor, whose influence is imperishable. The birth of Jesus Christ was the coming of *God* into this world. We all stand with uncovered head beside the manger in the little town of Bethlehem, for he who sleeps his first sleep there, is Emmanuel—God with us. That is why we write *Anno Domini* in all our dates. These are years of our Lord. Whatever of good, beauty, joy, and hope there was in the centuries before Jesus was born, it was indeed a new beginning of time when he came.

We need not say that this was not God's world before Christ came. "The earth is the Lord's and the fullness thereof." Nor is it true that he was not in it then. The Old Testament tells of divine appearances. But they were rare, and gave scarcely more than*glimpses* of ineffable presence. There were divine revealings—but they were only *flashes* or *gleams* of glory. We do well to reckon time from the birth of Jesus Christ, for in his incarnation all the fullness of the divine life was brought down among men.

We may say, for example, that *love* was given a new meaning when Jesus came into this world. Of course, there was love here before. Mothers loved their children. Friend loved friend. Some of the rarest friendships of history, belong n the centuries before the beginning of the Christian era. But Jesus illustrated in his life, the love which reaches out beyond all lines of kinship and natural affection. "What do you do more than others?" was the test question the Master put to his disciples. Anybody can love his friends, and be kind to those who are kind to him, and graciously greet those who greet him. Even the heathen loved in this way. Jesus said, "I say unto you, Love your *enemies*, and pray for those who *persecute* you; that you may be sons of your Father who is in heaven." Forgiving injuries is not an expression of natural affection—but the love which Jesus taught prays, "Forgive us—as we forgive others."

The ancient law said, "You shall love your neighbor as yourself"; Christ law of love requires, not "as yourself," but more than we love ourselves. We are to give our own life, if need be, in love's service. The parable of the Good Samaritan is our Lord's own illustration of the way we are to love our neighbor. He may be an enemy—it was so in the story—but the man who did us a cruel wrong yesterday, if we find him in need today—is our neighbor. The love we are to show is not merely *pity*— but *help*to the uttermost, whatever the cost may be.

But a lofty teaching was not all that Jesus brought to earth. People might have said that no one could live up to the standards which he gave, that no one could realize the splendid ideals of his teaching. But Jesus lived up to his own standards, and realized every one of his own ideals. He brought into the world, not merely new interpretations of the duty of loving—he brought *love itself!* Some scientific men, in trying to account for the beginning of vegetable life in this world, have suggested that possibly some fragment of a bursting planet may have been hurled to our globe, bringing with it its roots and seeds, and that thus life began here. We need not give the fancy any thought—but it illustrates the way love came to our earth. Out of heaven came One who himself was the infinite and eternal Love. In bringing life, he brought love—for life is love, and love is life. All the love that is in this world today, and all that has been here since Christ was born, was kindled from the one flame which burned in the heart of Jesus.

For not only was he the very love of God brought to earth in the incarnation—but he came to give that same love to others, to put it into the heart of everyone who would believe on him. It is not impossible for men, therefore, to attain the lofty standards of living which Jesus gave for his friends. He came not to teach lessons merely—but to give life—and to give it abundantly.

Everyone who touched Jesus, carried away in his own heart a new warmth, which by and by transformed his life. Then everyone whose life was kindled at this flame of love, in turn kindled other lives. So the work has gone on through these nineteen centuries. Through all human strifes and contentions, amid cruelty, injustice, and oppression, love has wrought persistently, winning its victories. Everyone who endures wrong patiently, who keeps his heart sweet under harshness or insult—is helping in the *triumph of love*. Everyone who does a kindly deed, makes the wintry air a little warmer.

It is such deeds as these, which are the truest interpretation of the love which had its earthly incarnation that first Christmas night. We can best prepare for the coming of the kingdom of Christ in its full glory, by letting love have its victories in us over all that might make us bitter or resentful—the love which bears all things and endures all things, and by doing ever the gentle deeds which comfort lonely hearts and relive suffering and distress.

We can make Christmas worthy of its sacred meaning, only by love. We need not seek far for opportunities—all about us are those whose hearts we can warm, whose lives we can inspire and enrich, simply by bringing to them the love of Christ.

Christmas After Christmas Day

What becomes of Christmas, when the day is gone? It is the gladdest day of the year. It is celebrated in all Christian lands. The churches observe it, sometimes with great pomp and splendor, with stately music and elaborate ceremonial, sometimes in simple, homely worship. It is kept in homes, with happy greetings and good wishes, and universal giving of gifts. Everyone, even the miser, grows generous at the Christmas time. Men who are ordinarily cold and unmoved toward human need, wax warm-hearted in these glad days. People everywhere rise to a high tide of kindly feeling. There is scarcely a home anywhere, however lowly, which the

Christmas sentiment does not reach with its kindliness. Public institutions—orphanages, hospitals, homes, prisons, refuges, reformatories—all feel themselves touched as by a breath of heaven, for the one day.

What becomes of all the joy when Christmas is over? Does it stay in the life of the community afterward? Do we have it in our homes the next day and the next week? Do we feel it in the atmosphere of our churches? Does it stay in the hearts of people in general? Do the carols sing on next day? Does the generous kindness continue in the people's hearts? Does the love in homes rich and poor abide through the winter?

Two or three years ago, in one of our cities, an Oriental was giving his impressions of our American Christmas. He said that for weeks before Christmas, people's faces seemed to have an unusual light in them. They were all bright and shining. Everyone seemed unusually kindly and courteous. Everyone was more thoughtful, more desirous of giving pleasure than had been his accustomed. Men who at other season of the year had been stern, unapproachable, were now genial, hearty, easy to approach. Those who ordinarily were stingy, not responding to calls for charity, had become, for the time, generous and charitable. Those who had been in the habit of doing base things, when they entered the warm Christmas zone seemed like new men, as if a new spirit possessed them. And the Oriental said it would be a good thing if all the charm of the Christmas spirit, could be made to project itself into the New Year.

This is really the problem to be solved. Christmas ought not to be one day only in the year—it should be all the days through the year. We may as well confess that the solution has not yet been realized. Almost immediately after Christmas, we fall back into a selfish way of living which is far below the high tide to which we rose at Christmas. There is a picture which shows the scene of our Lord's crucifixion in the afternoon of that terrible day. The crowd is gone, the crosses are empty, and all is silent. In the background is seen a donkey nibbling at a piece of withered palm branch. This was all that was left of the joy and enthusiasm of Psalm Sunday.

Is it not much the same with the beautiful life of Christmas? Five days afterward, will not the world have gone back to its old coldness, selfishness, and hardness? Will not the newspapers have resumed the story of wrong, injustice, greed, and crime, just as if there had been no Christmas, with its one day's peace and good will? Shall we not have again about us, within a few days, the old competition, wrangling, strife and bitterness among men? The sweet flowers of Christmas will soon be found trampled in the dust by the same feet which, this Christmas, are standing by the cradle of the Christ-child.

How can we keep the Christmas spirit with us after the day has passed on the calendar? We cannot legislate a continuation of Christmas good will. We cannot extend it by passing resolutions. We cannot hold it in the world's life by lecturing and exhorting on the subject. Yet there ought to be some way of making Christmas last more than one day. It is too beautiful to be allowed to fade out after only one brief day's stay in the world. What can we do to extend it? We can begin by keeping the beautiful vision in our own life.

There is a story of a young woman who had been with an outing party all day. In the morning, as she left her home, almost unconsciously she had slipped a branch of sweetbrier into her dress. She altogether forgot that it was there. All day, wherever she went with her friends, she and others smelled the spicy fragrance—but none knew whence it came. Yet that night, when she went to her room there was the handful of sweetbrier tucked away in her dress, where she had put it in the morning, and where, unconsciously, she had carried it all day.

The secret was revealed. It is when we have the sweetness in our own life, that we begin to be a sweetener of other lives. We cannot depend upon others for our Christ-likeness, but if we have it in our own heart we will impart it to those about us. We cannot find sweetness on every path that our feet must press. Sometimes we must be among uncongenial people, people whose lives are not loving, with whom it is not easy to live cordially in close relations. The only way to be sure of making all our course in life a path of sweetness is to have the fragrance in ourselves. Then on bleakest roads, where not a flower blooms, we still shall walk in perfumed air— the perfume being in our hearts. It is our own heart which makes our world. We find everywhere what we take with us. If our lives are gentle, patient, loving—we find gentleness, patience, lovingness everywhere. But if our hearts are bitter, jealous, suspicious—we find bitterness, jealousy, suspicion, on every path.

Shall we not strive to make Christmas a continual festival, and not merely the festival of one day? This does not mean a constant celebration of the outer life of Christmas—but a continuance of its spirit.

Henry Van Dyke puts it thus: "Are you willing to stoop down to consider the needs and the desires of little children; to remember the weakness and loneliness of people who are growing old; to stop asking how much your friends love you, and ask yourself whether you love them enough; to bear in mind the things that other people have to bear in mind—the things that other people have to bear on their hearts; to try to understand what those who live in the same house with you really want, without waiting for them to tell you; to trim your lamp so that it will give more light and less smoke; to make a grave for your ugly thoughts, and a garden for your kindly feelings, with the gate open? Are you willing to do these things even for a day? Then you can keep Christmas."

And when we are doing these things every day, Christmas will have fulfilled its mission.

The Problem of Christian Old Age

"Therefore we do not lose heart. Though outwardly we are wasting away, yet inwardly we are being renewed day by day!" 2 Corinthians 4:16. Paul has a cheering thought about the undecaying inner life. The outward man, he says, *always decays*—but the inner man is renewed day by day. This teaching is full of comfort for those who are advancing in years. The problem of *Christian old age*—is to keep the heart young and full of all youth's joy, however feeble and broken the body may become. We need to be most watchful lest we allow our life to lose its zest and deteriorate in its quality, when old age begins to creep in. Hopes of achievement appear to be ended for us—our work is almost done, we think. Sometimes people, as they grow old, become less sweet, less beautiful in spirit. Troubles, disasters, and misfortunes have made the days hard and painful for them. Perhaps health is broken, and *suffering* is added to the other elements which make old age unhappy.

Renan, in one of his books, recalls an old legend of buried city on the coast of Brittany. With its homes, public buildings, churches and thronged streets—it sank instantly into the sea. The legend says that the city's life goes on as before, down beneath the waves. The fishermen, when in calm weather they row over the place, think they sometimes can see the gleaming tips of the church spires deep in the water, and fancy they can hear the chiming of the bells in the old belfries and even the murmur of the city's noises.

There are men who in their old age seem to have an experience like this. Their life of youthful hopes, dreams, successes, loves and joys, has been sunk out of sight, submerged in misfortunes and adversities, and has vanished altogether. Nothing remains of it all but a *memory*. In their discouragement they often think sadly of their past, and seem to hear the echoes of the old songs of hope and joy, and to catch visions of the old beauty and splendor. But that is all. Nothing real is left. Their spirits have grown hopeless and bitter. Guthrie, as he grew feeble, spoke of his bald head, his trembling steps, his dullness of hearing, his dimness of eye.

But this is not *worthy living,* for those who are immortal, who were born to be children of God. The hard things are not meant to mar our life—they are meant to make us only the braver, the worthier, and the nobler. It is not meant that the *infirmities of old age* shall break through into our inner life; that should grow all the more beautiful—the more the outer life is broken. The shattering of the old mortal tent, should reveal more and more of the glory of the divine life which dwells within.

Do you ever think, you who are growing old, that old age ought really to be the very best of life? We are too apt to settle down to the feeling, that with our infirmities, we cannot any longer live beautifully, worthily, usefully, or actively. But this is not the true way to think of old age. We should reach our best then in every way.

Old age should be the best—the very best, of all life! It should be the most beautiful, with the *flaws* mended, the *faults* cured, the *mistakes* corrected, the *lessons* learned. Youth is full of immaturity. Midlife is full of toil and care, strife and ambition. Old age should be as the autumn with its golden fruit. We ought to be better Christians than ever we have been before; more submissive to God's will; more content, more patient and gentle, kindlier and more loving—when we grow old. We are drawing nearer to heaven every day—and our visions of the Father's house should be clearer and brighter. Old age is the time of harvest; it should not be marked by emptiness and decay—but by richer fruitfulness and more gracious beauty. It may be lonely, with so many gone of those who used to cluster about the life—but the loneliness will not be for long, for it is drawing nearer continually to all the great company of godly friends, waiting in heaven.

Old age may be feeble—but the marks of feebleness are really foretokens of glory. Old people have no reason for sadness—they are really in their *best* days! Let them be sure to live now at their best. Paul was growing old when he wrote of his enthusiastic vision of beauty yet to be attained—but we hear no note of depression or weariness in him. He did not think of his life as done. He showed no consciousness that he had passed the highest reach of living. He was still forgetting the past and reaching forth, because he knew that the best was yet before him. His outward man was feeble, his health shattered, his physical vigor decaying—but the inner man was undecayed and undecaying. He was never before so Christ-like as he was now, never so full of hope, never so enthusiastic in his service of his Master.

Those who are growing old should show the ripest spiritual fruitfulness. They should do their best work for Christ in the days which remain. They should live their sweetest, gentlest, kindliest, most helpful life in the short time which they have yet to remain in this world. They should make their years of old age—years of quietness and peace, and joy—a holy eventide. But this can be the story of their experiences only if their life be hid with Christ in God. Apart from Christ, no life can keep its zest or its radiance.

Made in the USA
Monee, IL
15 December 2019